SOUTH LANCASHIRE TROLLEYBUSES

Stephen Lockwood

MP Middleton Press

Front cover: Karrier/Sunbeam MS2 no 70 stands at Bolton Bus Station before departing for Leigh. (R Marshall)

Rear cover upper: An example of a South Lancashire trolleybus Fare Stage sign. (A.P.Tyldsley coll.)

Rear cover lower: Three trolleybuses are seen at the Leigh terminus in 1956. From left to right are Leyland no 57 on the Bolton service, Guy four wheeler no 45 bound for Mosley Common, and 'utility' Karrier no 62 working back to Atherton depot. No 45, thirty-three years old, has a grey roof with white bands. Note that all the vehicles have differing styles of fleet number display, and that the registration letters shown by no 62 - 'FDT' are incorrect and should be 'FTD', a very short lived error. (C.Carter, colour added by Malcolm Fraser)

ABBREVIATIONS AND GLOSSARY

SLT The South Lancashire Transport Company
LUT The Lancashire United Transport (and Power) Company
BUT British United Traction
GEC General Electric Company

Lowbridge   A type of bus bodywork construction that produced a body lower than a conventional bus body, enabling operation under some low bridges. This was achieved by having a sunken gangway on the upper deck, with seats arranged in long benches. The sunken gangway intruded into the lower saloon, reducing the headroom for passengers on one side. On a trolleybus the height of such a vehicle was about 14 feet. Highbridge trolleybuses, with conventional seating on the upper deck, had a height of around 15 feet.

Ownership of overhead wiring (to the nearest mile)
SLT   27
St Helens Corporation   4
Bolton Corporation   3
Farnworth Corporation   2 (maintained by SLT)

Published October 2012

ISBN 978 1 908174 30 7

© Middleton Press, 2012

Design Deborah Esher

Published by
　　　Middleton Press
　　　Easebourne Lane
　　　Midhurst
　　　West Sussex
　　　GU29 9AZ
Tel: 01730 813169
Fax: 01730 812601
Email: info@middletonpress.co.uk
www.middletonpress.co.uk

Printed in the United Kingdom by Henry Ling Limited, at the Dorset Press, Dorchester, DT1 1HD

CONTENTS

The routes
    The Atherton hub   1
    West to St Helens   14
    East to Swinton   32
    Swinton to Farnworth   61
    South to Leigh   75
    North to Bolton   90

The vehicles   108
    Testing times   117
    Finale   119

INTRODUCTION AND ACKNOWLEDGEMENTS

    It is no exaggeration to describe the trolleybus system operating between 1930 and 1958 in the industrial towns of south-east Lancashire as extraordinary. South Lancashire Transport (SLT) was a company owned operation of 71 trolleybuses running over 36 miles of route. The operating hub of the system was situated in the relatively small town of Atherton. These routes connected to larger towns on the edges of Manchester and Liverpool and were some of the longest in the country, wending their way, often an indirect one, through the coal mining and cotton spinning communities. Each of the largest of the towns they reached, Bolton, Leigh and St Helens, had its own municipal motorbus system, but only the last named ran trolleybuses. The situation in Leigh was unique because the local municipal bus operator had no involvement with the trolleybus route running into the centre of its town, either by running vehicles or owning overhead. Most of the SLT vehicles in the later days of operation were veritable antiques, some of the oldest dating from the opening of the system in 1930. One observer described to me recently about these veterans: 'They growled around as if their working parts were filled with sand'.

    In this volume, the reader is taken on a virtual ride on all these routes as they were in the final days of their life, the mid-1950s. Very few of the photographs date from before this time. Thus this is not primarily an historical work, but an impression of what the SLT trolleybuses were like on the streets, as well as capturing the shops, fashions and other road vehicles of the time. Readers requiring additional historical background are directed to the late EK Stretch's history 'South Lancashire Tramways', published in 1972, and Phillip Taylor's 2002 book entitled 'A Trolleybus to the Punch Bowl'. Both works have been referred to in the preparation of this book. Since these were published, some very significant photographic collections of SLT trolleybuses have become available, and I have sought to include as many of these as possible. Notable are the photographs of the late Roy Brook, of which no less than thirty are included herein. Although primarily a tram enthusiast, Roy took many photographs of British trolleybus systems, but the one he took most images of, apart from his native Huddersfield, was South Lancashire, a reflection, no doubt, of the fondness he had for the system. I am grateful to Paul Watson for the loan of all Roy's SLT photographs.

    My thanks also go to Colin Barker, Ron Barton, Peter Caunt, Hugh Davies of 'Photos from the Fifties', Michael Dryhurst, John Fozard, David Hall of the British Trolleybus Society, Martin Jenkins of the Online Transport Archive, Don Jones, John Kaye, Stanley King, Alex Millar of Wigan Archive Service, Douglas Parker, Robin Symons of the Trolleybus Museum Company, Hugh Taylor, Peter Thompson, Tony Wilson of Travel Lens Photographic, and Colin Wright for willingly agreeing to supply photographic material and to Roger Smith for drawing the excellent and extensive maps of the system. I am also grateful to Stanley King, Jim Saunders, Phillip Taylor and Andrew Tyldsley for checking the text and suggesting amendments and clarifications, to Eric Old who has supplied the tickets and Andrew Tyldsley for the timetable extracts and 'Fare Stage' plate: also Malcolm Fraser for colouring the photograph shown on the rear cover. Finally, I need to thank my wife Eileen for her constant support and critical eye on my efforts.

Regarding photographic credits - except where noted:
  Photographs credited to Roy Brook are courtesy of Paul Watson.
  Photographs credited to J Copland are courtesy of David Packer.
  Photographs credited to DA Jones are courtesy of the London Trolleybus Preservation Society
  All the photographs credited to JS King were taken by him on Sunday 24th March 1957.

The timetable extracts inserted throughout the book show details of the main services operated during 1956. Note that each one uses a different interpretation of the word 'trolleybus'.

GEOGRAPHICAL AND HISTORICAL SETTING

As the company name implies, the area operated by the SLT, was, during the lifetime of the trolleybus system, in Lancashire. Today this area is in the conurbation of Greater Manchester, apart from the outer end of the former St Helens route which is now in Merseyside. This was part of the Lancashire coalfield, and many of the communities that the trolleybuses passed through had mining origins. Cotton processing and iron industries also prevailed. There is a rich theme of transport history in the area. The canal era was founded in the 18th century at Worsley Delph, very close to the future trolleybus route, where the beginnings of the Bridgewater Canal were constructed to transport coal. The first main line railway, opened in 1830 between Manchester and Liverpool, ran to the south of the area. An equivalent motor highway, the East Lancashire Road (A580) opened in 1934, crossed the trolleybus routes in several places.

HISTORICAL BACKGROUND

The South Lancashire Transport Company came into being following the passing of The South Lancashire Transport Bill in May 1929. This empowered the South Lancashire Tramways Company to change its name, substituting 'Transport' for 'Tramways' in its title, and to authorise the introduction of Trolley Vehicles to replace trams over the SLT routes. The SLT Company was a subsidiary of the Lancashire United Transport and Power Company, which ran motorbus services in the area. Its name was changed to the Lancashire United Transport Company in 1948, following the nationalisation of its power generation activities which up to this date supplied the trolleybus network from the Atherton Howe Bridge power station.

Accordingly, on 3rd August 1930, ten Guy six-wheel trolleybuses with Roe lowbridge bodies entered service between Atherton and Ashton in Makerfield, replacing trams on that section. This was to be part of the route to St Helens, a joint operation with St Helens Corporation, but the construction of the East Lancashire Road over the route beyond Ashton delayed the inauguration of the full service, which eventually opened through to St Helens on 21st June 1931.

Shortly afterwards, on 19th August 1931, the long route from Atherton, via Swinton to Farnworth was converted to trolleybus operation, and a further 19 Guy trolleybuses were put into service, with an additional one following in November, giving a fleet total of thirty vehicles.

The next route to be converted to trolleybuses was that between Leigh and Bolton. The Leigh route trams ran beyond Leigh to Lowton St Marys, but the portion south of Leigh town centre was not equipped for trolleybus operation and the trams on that section were replaced by LUT motorbuses. Trolleybuses took over operation of the Leigh to Bolton route on 17th December 1933. The last SLT tram had run on the previous evening, although the company continued to maintain sections of tramway in the Farnworth area which were used by Bolton Corporation trams until 1944. Sixteen Guy four-wheel trolleybuses were provided for the new trolleybus route, these naturally being smaller than the previous vehicles.

Bolton Corporation owned and maintained the trolleybus overhead between Four Lane Ends and Bolton, and continued to run the local tram service from there into Bolton on the same route as the trolleybuses. However, from 29th March 1936, SLT trolleybuses replaced the Bolton trams on these local journeys under a financial arrangement with the Corporation. Bolton paid SLT the cost of purchasing four additional vehicles to run the service, these being highbridge Leylands, and only when these were fully depreciated would they nominally become the property of the Corporation. Despite this, the vehicles concerned were not confined to operating this local service and ran on all routes available to highbridge vehicles as part of the normal fleet.

The trolleybus system was now at its maximum extent. The St Helens and Swinton/Farnworth routes were very long at approximately 14 miles each (although the distance between Atherton and Farnworth was only six miles by the shortest road route). These routes passed through industrial colliery landscape, although some more pleasant rural terrain was traversed east of Boothstown and at Worsley, both on the way to Swinton. There were frequent turning facilities along the way, usually in the form of a detached reversing triangle (ie without frogs), although, especially due to difficulties during the wartime blackout, most of these had been improved with pointwork being inserted by the post-war period. SLT erected its own trolleybus wiring, rather than using a contractor, and merely used the existing tram bracket arms to support 18 inch spaced overhead using tramway fittings. This approach also applied to any special work, such as frogs and crossings instead of using pre-fabricated assemblies. Only the Leigh to Bolton route used span wiring to the more modern 24" spacing, although sections of other routes were subsequently modernised. There were three depots, at Atherton (Howe Bridge), Platt Bridge and Swinton.

Eight more six-wheel Leylands entered service in 1937 and 1938, and increased passenger traffic during the war resulted in six Karrier four-wheelers, built to the standard Ministry of Transport 'utility' specification, joining the fleet in 1943-4. A further six Karrier / Sunbeam six-wheelers came in 1948, these being the last trolleybuses purchased, although it is of note that , although one vehicle was withdrawn from service in 1951, it was not until 1955 that any significant reduction of the fleet took place.

By 1950, the following services were being worked on a daily basis:

Atherton - St Helens (joint with St Helens Corporation)
Atherton - Swinton - Farnworth
Bolton - Atherton - Leigh
Leigh - Atherton - Mosley Common
Bolton - Hulton Lane (extended to Four Lane Ends at peak hours)

In addition, on weekdays an additional service ran between Farnworth and Swinton only, and at works times and Saturdays many unadvertised extras (known as 'jiggers' to the crews) ran throughout the system, many using the various intermediate turning circles and reversing triangles.

The long Atherton- Farnworth route was operated in two overlapping sections (Atherton to Swinton and Worsley to Farnworth), although the vehicles worked throughout and passengers had to re-book at Swinton. Passengers on the Bolton route riding through the Atherton / Bolton boundary at Four Lane Ends also had to re-book, and conductors were required to carry separate ticket stocks (later separate ticket machines) for use in each section on this route.

In this post-war period, many of the lowbridge trolleybuses were modernised in varying degrees, ranging from new dash panels to complete new fronts or total body rebuilding. However in August 1955, the decision was made to replace trolleybuses with motorbuses. The Bolton local service ran for the last time on 25th March 1956, and the four Leyland trolleybuses now nominally owned by Bolton Corporation, passed to that authority for disposal. On Sunday 11th November 1956, the St Helens route was converted, although the wiring and trolleybuses withdrawn from service were retained for some months on the instructions of the Ministry of Transport, due to the Suez oil crisis. Services on the other routes, to Farnworth and Leigh – Bolton continued until 1958, the latter having a stay of execution whilst a dispute with Leigh Corporation over the bus route licensing arrangements was settled. In 1958, a bill was passed in Parliament (The South Lancashire Transport Act 1958) which authorised the abandonment of the system in favour of Lancashire United motorbuses. The St Helens trolleybus route closure had been achieved by using mainly motorbuses with SLT legal lettering. Also authorised in the bill was the dissolution of the South Lancashire Transport Company. Thus, Sunday 31st August 1958 was the last day for the operation of the remaining trolleybus routes, and for the Company itself. A formal ceremony took place the following day, including a short run by a trolleybus displaying suitable 'Last Trolleybus' signage and legal lettering for the Lancashire United Transport Company.

SOUTH LANCASHIRE TRANSPORT Co. Ltd.
TROLLEYBUS ROUTES
Map 1a Location

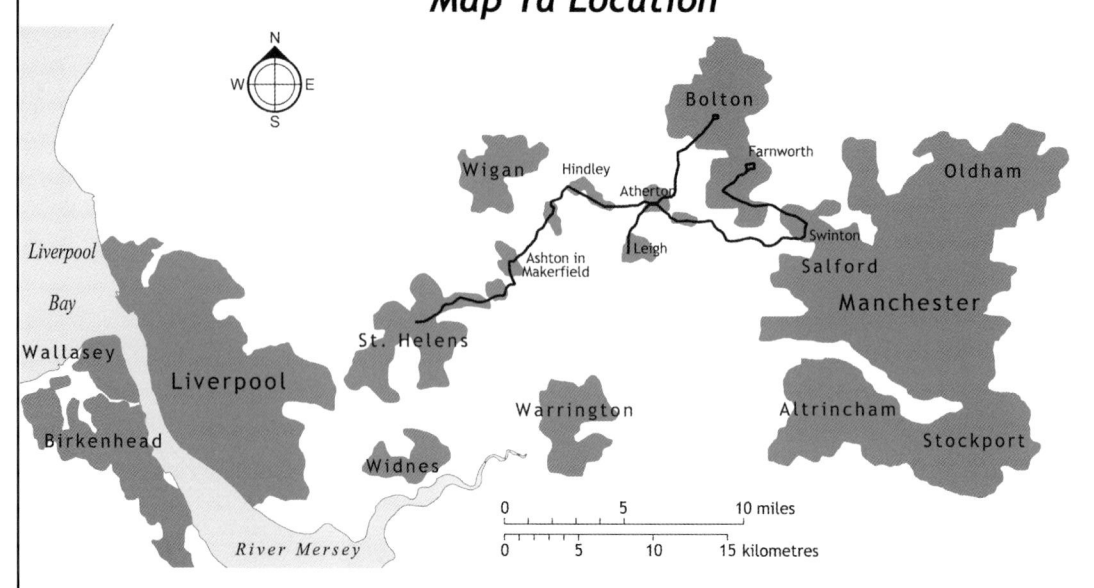

TROLLEYBUS ROUTES
Map 1b Key to Detail Maps

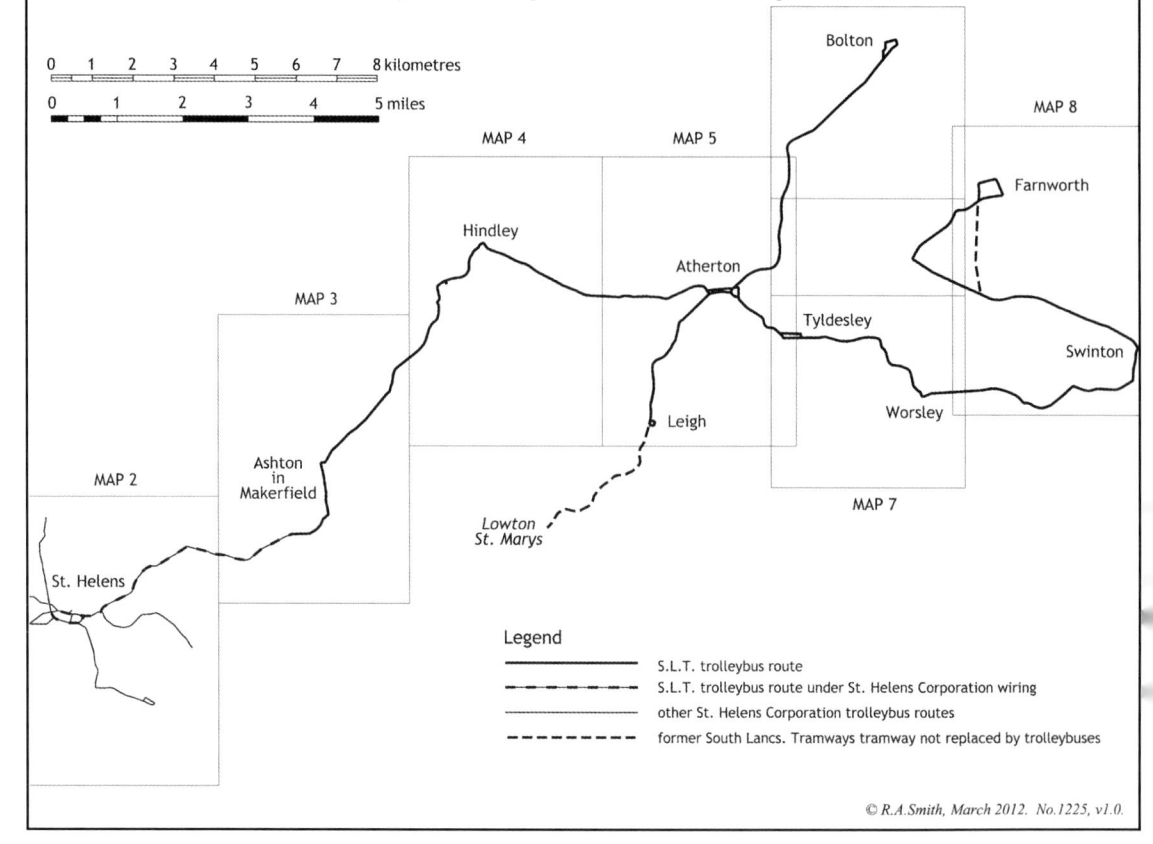

Legend

————————	S.L.T. trolleybus route
– – – – – – –	S.L.T. trolleybus route under St. Helens Corporation wiring
————————	other St. Helens Corporation trolleybus routes
▬ ▬ ▬ ▬ ▬ ▬	former South Lancs. Tramways tramway not replaced by trolleybuses

© R.A.Smith, March 2012. No.1225, v1.0.

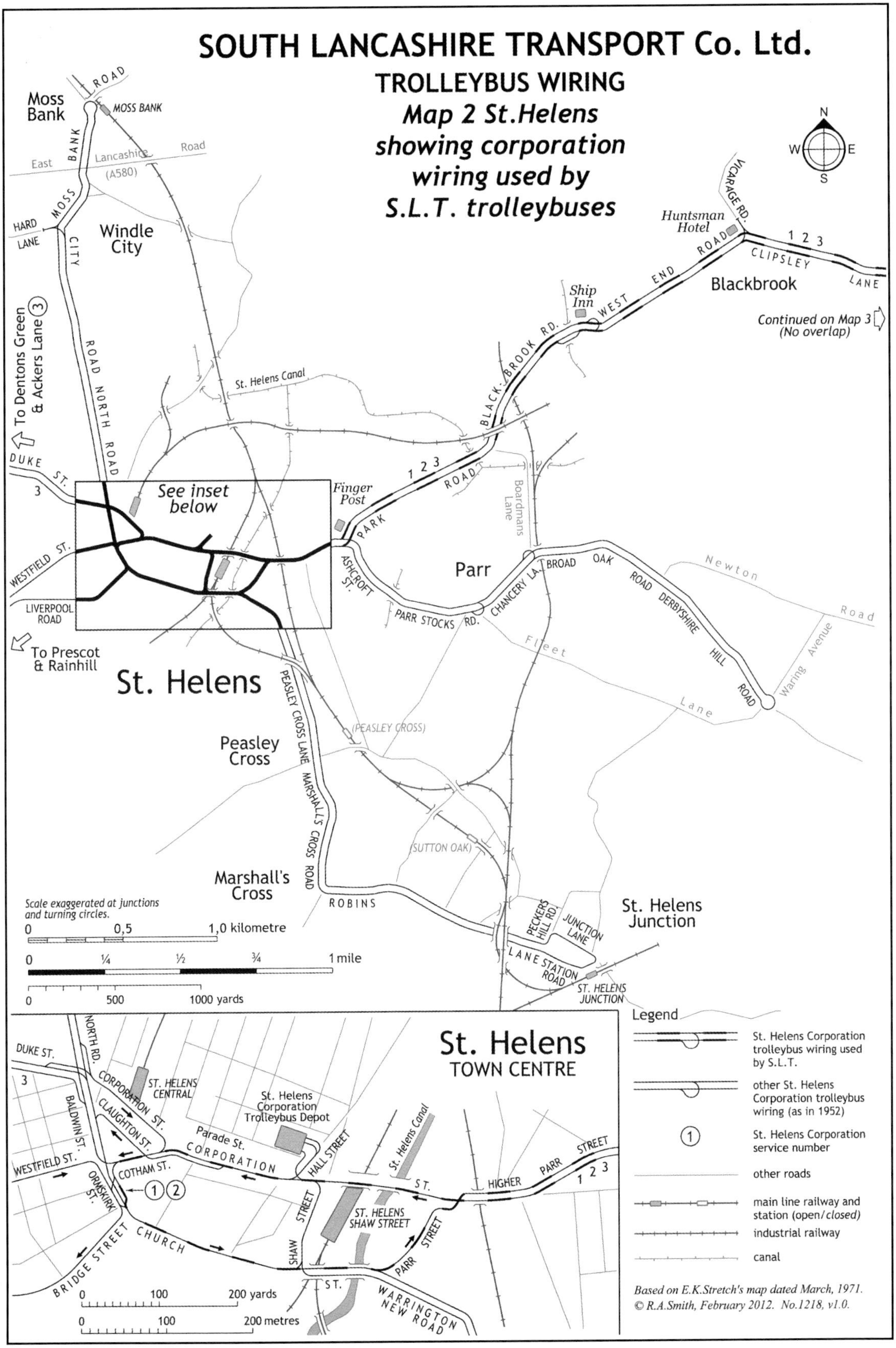
SOUTH LANCASHIRE TRANSPORT Co. Ltd.
TROLLEYBUS WIRING
Map 2 St.Helens showing corporation wiring used by S.L.T. trolleybuses
N
W
E
S
Moss Bank
ROAD
MOSS BANK
East Lancashire Road
(A580)
MOSS BANK
HARD LANE
CITY
Windle City
To Dentons Green & Ackers Lane 3
ROAD NORTH ROAD
DUKE ST.
3
St. Helens Canal
See inset below
WESTFIELD ST.
LIVERPOOL ROAD
To Prescot & Rainhill
St. Helens
Finger Post
PARK ROAD
1 2 3
BLACKBROOK RD.
Ship Inn
WEST END ROAD
Huntsman Hotel
VICARAGE RD.
CLIPSLEY LANE
1 2 3
Blackbrook
Continued on Map 3 (No overlap)
Boardmans Lane
ASHCROFT ST.
PARR STOCKS RD.
Parr
CHANCERY LA.
BROAD OAK ROAD
DERBYSHIRE HILL ROAD
Newton Road
Waring Avenue
Fleet Lane
PEASLEY CROSS LANE
(PEASLEY CROSS)
Peasley Cross
MARSHALL'S CROSS ROAD
(SUTTON OAK)
Marshall's Cross
ROBINS LANE
PECKERS HILL RD.
JUNCTION LANE
STATION ROAD
St. Helens Junction
ST. HELENS JUNCTION
Scale exaggerated at junctions and turning circles.
0 0,5 1,0 kilometre
0 ¼ ½ ¾ 1 mile
0 500 1000 yards
St. Helens TOWN CENTRE
DUKE ST.
NORTH RD.
3
CORPORATION ST.
ST. HELENS CENTRAL
CLAUGHTON ST.
BALDWIN ST.
WESTFIELD ST.
COTHAM ST.
ORMSKIRK ST.
1 2
Parade St.
CORPORATION
St. Helens Corporation Trolleybus Depot
HALL STREET
St. Helens Canal
ST.
HIGHER PARR STREET
1 2 3
SHAW STREET
ST. HELENS SHAW STREET
PARR STREET
CHURCH
BRIDGE STREET
ST.
WARRINGTON NEW ROAD
0 100 200 yards
0 100 200 metres
Legend
St. Helens Corporation trolleybus wiring used by S.L.T.
other St. Helens Corporation trolleybus wiring (as in 1952)
1 St. Helens Corporation service number
other roads
main line railway and station (open/closed)
industrial railway
canal
Based on E.K.Stretch's map dated March, 1971.
© R.A.Smith, February 2012. No.1218, v1.0.

SOUTH LANCASHIRE TRANSPORT Co. Ltd.
TROLLEYBUS WIRING
Map 3 Ashton in Makerfield

Continued on Map 4 (No overlap)

Bamfurlong

LILY LANE

Bryn Gates

BOLTON ROAD

Mains Colliery

L.C.

Stubshaw Cross

Bryn Road

Golborne Road

Wigan Road

Ashton in Makerfield

Robin Hood

PRINCESS ROAD

②

Liverpool Road

GERARD STREET

WARRINGTON ROAD

ASHTON IN MAKERFIELD

LODGE LANE

LANE

1 2

Lodge Lane

KENYON LANE

Ram's Head

③ L.C.

East Lancs. Road (A580)

PENNY

St.H.C.T. / S.L.T. boundary

CHURCH ROAD

1 2 3

L.C.

CLIPSLEY LANE

HAYDOCK

Haydock Colliery

Haydock

Continued on Map 2 (No overlap)

Legend

══○══	S.L.T. trolleybus wiring
══○══	St. Helens Corporation trolleybus wiring used by S.L.T.
①	St. Helens Corporation service number
——	other roads
─┼─▭─┼─	main line railway and station (open/closed)
─┼┼┼┼┼─	industrial railway
────	canal
L.C.	level crossing

Scale exaggerated at junctions and turning circles.

0   0,5   1,0 kilometre
0   ¼   ½   ¾   1 mile
0   500   1000 yards

Based on E.K.Stretch's map dated March, 1971.
© R.A.Smith, February 2012. No.1219, v1.0.

SOUTH LANCASHIRE TRANSPORT Co. Ltd.
TROLLEYBUS WIRING
Map 4 Hindley

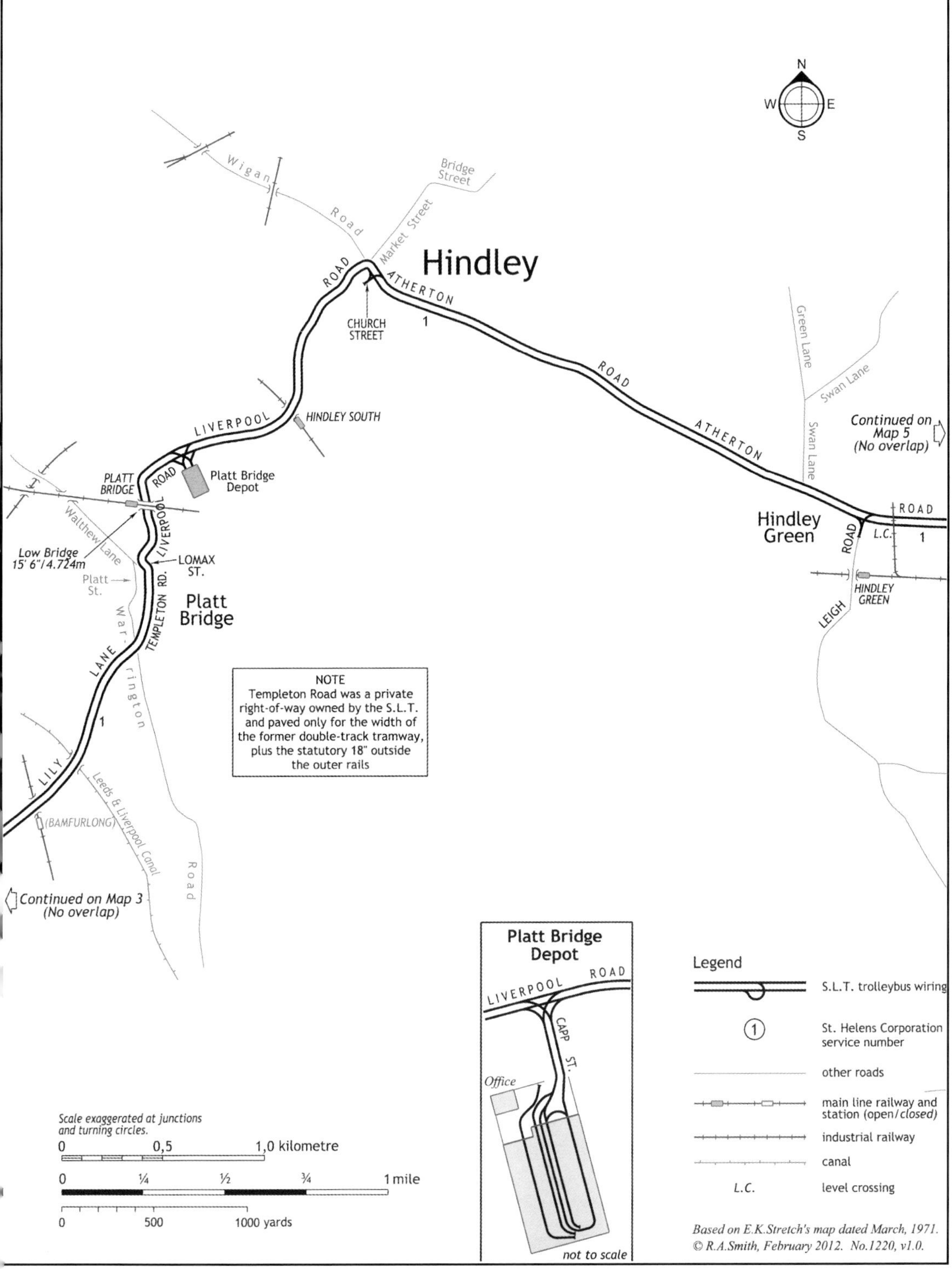

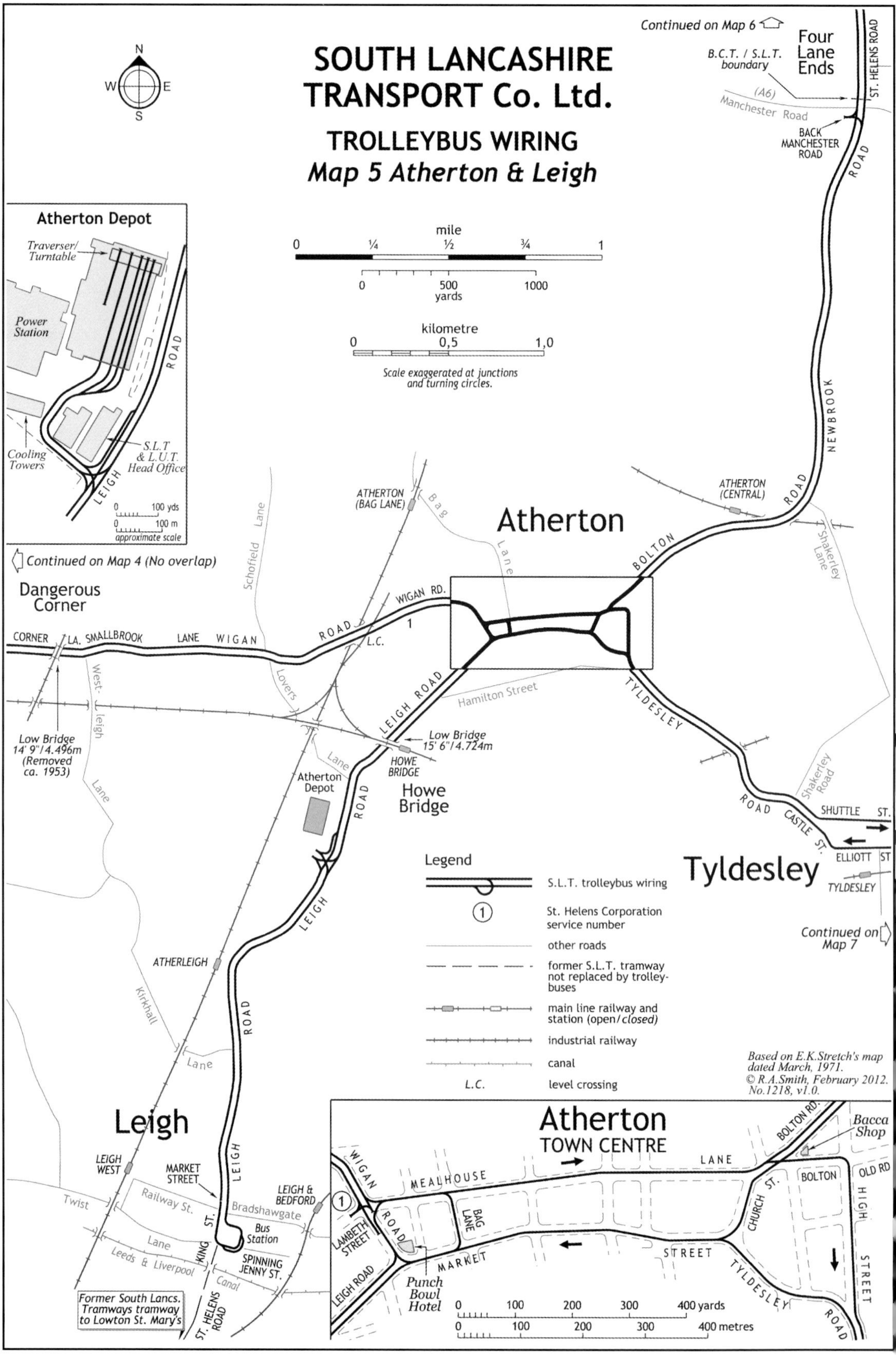
SOUTH LANCASHIRE TRANSPORT Co. Ltd.
TROLLEYBUS WIRING
Map 5 Atherton & Leigh
N
W
E
S
Continued on Map 6
Four Lane Ends
B.C.T. / S.L.T. boundary
(A6)
Manchester Road
BACK MANCHESTER ROAD
ST. HELENS ROAD
ROAD
NEWBROOK
ROAD
ATHERTON (CENTRAL)
Shakerley Lane
Atherton Depot
Traverser/ Turntable
Power Station
Cooling Towers
S.L.T & L.U.T. Head Office
ROAD
LEIGH
0
100 yds
0
100 m
approximate scale
mile
0
¼
½
¾
1
0
500
1000
yards
kilometre
0
0,5
1,0
Scale exaggerated at junctions and turning circles.
Continued on Map 4 (No overlap)
Dangerous Corner
CORNER
LA.
SMALLBROOK
LANE
WIGAN
ROAD
WIGAN RD.
1
L.C.
Schofield Lane
ATHERTON (BAG LANE)
Bag
Lane
Atherton
BOLTON
Lovers
Lane
West-leigh
Lane
Low Bridge 14' 9"/4.496m (Removed ca. 1953)
Hamilton Street
LEIGH ROAD
Low Bridge 15' 6"/4.724m
HOWE BRIDGE
Howe Bridge
Atherton Depot
ROAD
TYLDESLEY
ROAD
CASTLE ST.
Shakerley Road
SHUTTLE ST.
ELLIOTT ST
Tyldesley
TYLDESLEY
Continued on Map 7
LEIGH
ATHERLEIGH
Kirkhall
Lane
ROAD
Legend
S.L.T. trolleybus wiring
1
St. Helens Corporation service number
other roads
former S.L.T. tramway not replaced by trolley-buses
main line railway and station (open/closed)
industrial railway
canal
L.C.
level crossing
Based on E.K.Stretch's map dated March, 1971.
© R.A.Smith, February 2012. No.1218, v1.0.
Leigh
LEIGH WEST
MARKET STREET
LEIGH
LEIGH & BEDFORD
Twist
Railway St.
Bradshawgate
Bus Station
Lane
ST.
KING
SPINNING JENNY ST.
Leeds & Liverpool
Canal
Former South Lancs. Tramways tramway to Lowton St. Mary's
ST. HELENS ROAD
Atherton TOWN CENTRE
WIGAN
ROAD
1
MEALHOUSE
LANE
BOLTON RD.
Bacca Shop
OLD RD
BOLTON
HIGH STREET
CHURCH ST.
BAG LANE
LAMBETH STREET
LEIGH ROAD
MARKET
STREET
TYLDESLEY
ROAD
Punch Bowl Hotel
0
100
200
300
400 yards
0
100
200
300
400 metres

SOUTH LANCASHIRE TRANSPORT Co. Ltd.
TROLLEYBUS WIRING
Map 6 Bolton

Wiring between Four Lane Ends and Bolton owned and maintained by Bolton Corporation

Bolton

Deane Road

Cannon Street

Willows Lane

High St.

Daubhill

Burnden

Manchester Road

Hulton Lane

Deane Lane

RUMWORTH & DAUBHILL

Morris Green Lane

PERTH ST.
Reverser removed mid-1940s

Methurst Lane

Bolton TOWN CENTRE

ASHBURNER STREET

HOWELL CROFT STH.

Bus Station

MOOR LANE

MOOR STREET

BOLTON GT. MOOR STREET STATION

Deane Road

DERBY ST.

GREAT MOOR

Trinity Street

BOLTON TRINITY STREET STATION

0   100   200 yds
0   100   200 m

Plodder Lane

Plodder Lane

ST. HELENS ROAD

Manchester Road (A6)
BACK MANCHESTER ROAD

B.C.T. / S.L.T. boundary

Salford Road (A6)

Four Lane Ends

Continued on Map 8

Scale exaggerated at junctions and turning circles.

0   0,5   1,0 kilometre
0   ¼   ½   ¾   1 mile
0   500   1000 yards

S.L.T. / Farnworth Corporation boundary

BUCKLEY LANE

Low Bridge 15' 3"/4.648m

Manchester Road West

Little Hulton

CLEGG LANE

Armitage Ave.

MANCHESTER ROAD (A6)

LITTLE HULTON

Continued on Map 8

NEWBROOK ROAD

Shakerley Lane

Legend

━━━	S.L.T. trolleybus wiring
───	other roads
─┼─┼─	main line railway and station (open/closed)
┼┼┼┼┼	industrial railway
───	canal

Continued on Map 5

Based on E.K.Stretch's map dated March, 1971.
© R.A.Smith, February 2012. No.1221, v1.0.

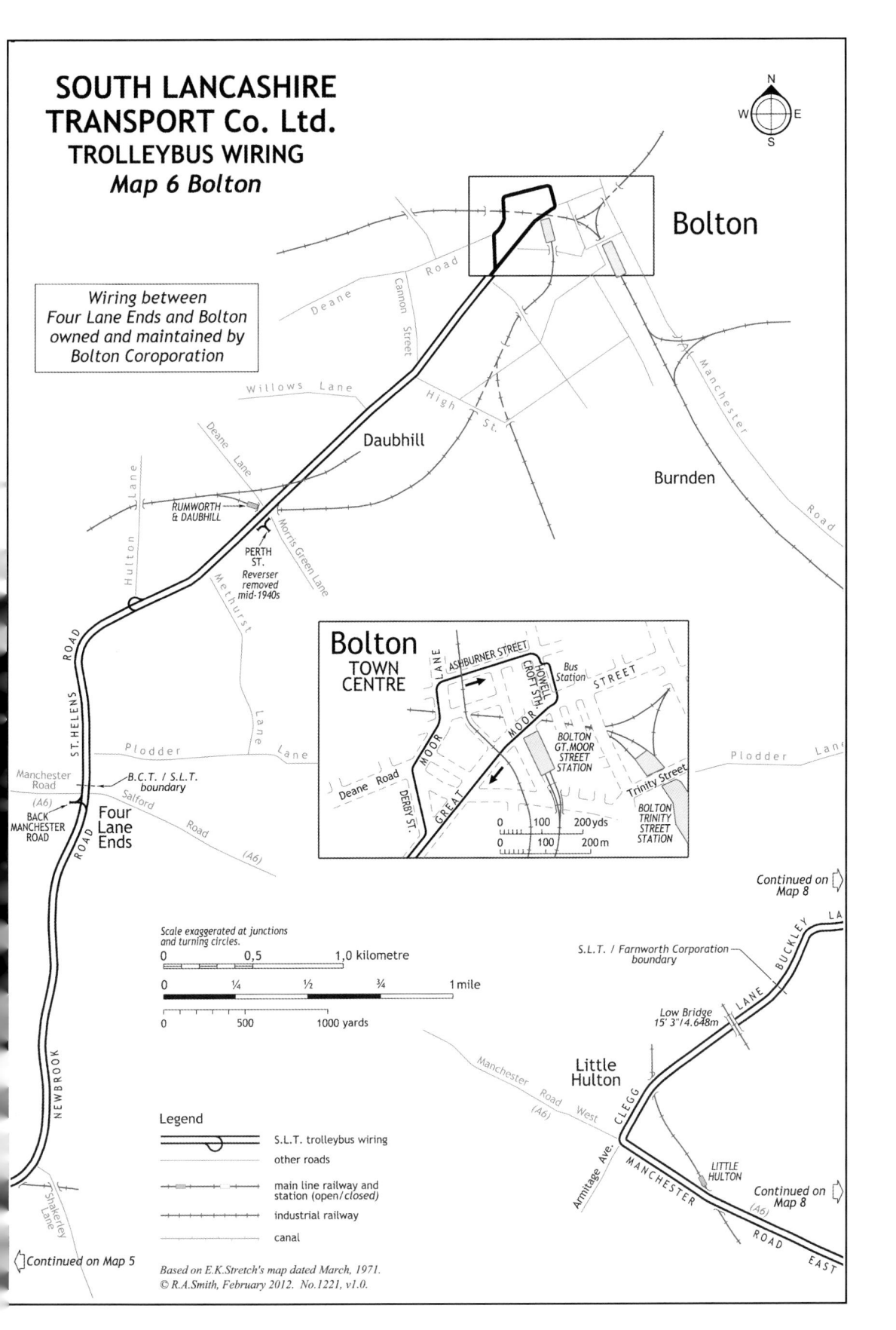

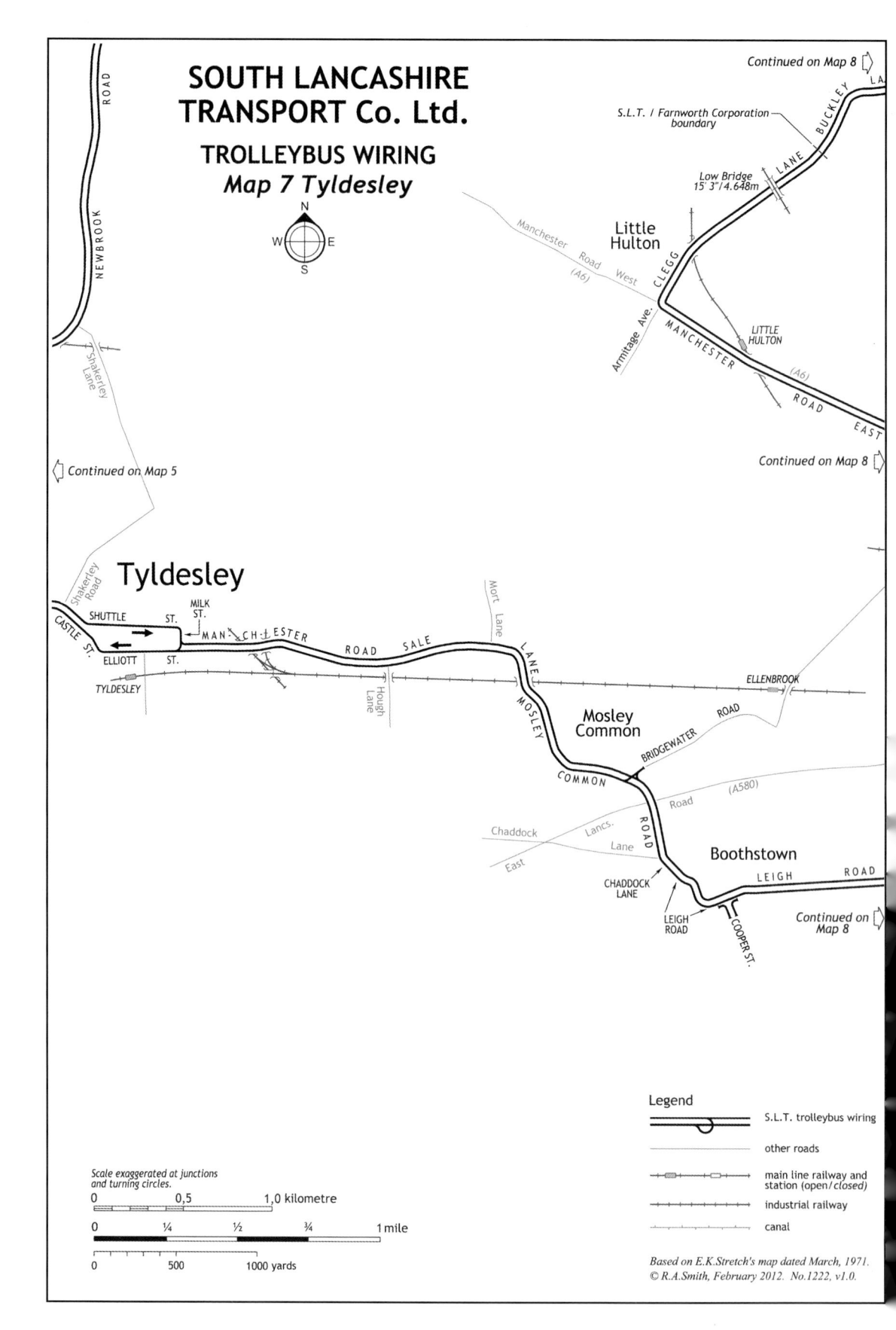

SOUTH LANCASHIRE TRANSPORT Co. Ltd.
TROLLEYBUS WIRING
Map 7 Tyldesley

SOUTH LANCASHIRE TRANSPORT Co. Ltd.
TROLLEYBUS WIRING
Map 8
Farnworth, Swinton & Worsley

Moses Gate

MOSES GATE

Egerton Street

Albert Street

Bolton Road

Market St.

FARNWORTH & HALSHAW MOOR

BRACKLEY ST.

HIGHER MARKET ST. (Kearsley)

MANCHESTER ROAD (Farnworth)

Farnworth

Black Horse

ALBERT ST.

LONG CAUSEWAY

OLD HALL ST.

Bolton Road

BUCKLEY LANE

WORSLEY ROAD NORTH

Bird i' th' Hand

Kearsley

Continued on Map 7

Wiring in Farnworth owned by Farnworth Corporation but maintained by S.L.T.

WORSLEY ROAD

BOLTON ROAD

Hill Top

Continued on Map 7

Walkden

'The Memorial'

Bridgewater Rd.

Memorial Road

MANCHESTER ROAD (A6)

WALKDEN (HIGH LEVEL)

WALKDEN (LOW LEVEL)

SANDHOLE LANE

MOORSIDE & WARDLEY

CHORLEY ROAD (A6)

Swinton

Swinton Church

VICARAGE ROAD

PARTINGTON LANE

Swinton Depot

Worsley Road

Folly Lane

East Lancs. Road (A580)

Walkden Road

Continued on Map 7

LEIGH ROAD

Worsley

WORSLEY BROW

'The Court House'

Bridgewater Canal

Bolton Rd.

WORSLEY ROAD

WORSLEY

Low Bridge 15' 6"/4.724m

Swinton Depot
not to scale

PARTINGTON LANE

Office

Legend

— S.L.T. trolleybus wiring

— other roads

— — — former S.L.T. tramway not replaced by trolley-buses

—■—■— main line railway and station (open/closed)

—+—+— industrial railway

———— canal

Based on E.K.Stretch's map dated March, 1971.
© R.A.Smith, February 2012. No.1223, v1.0.

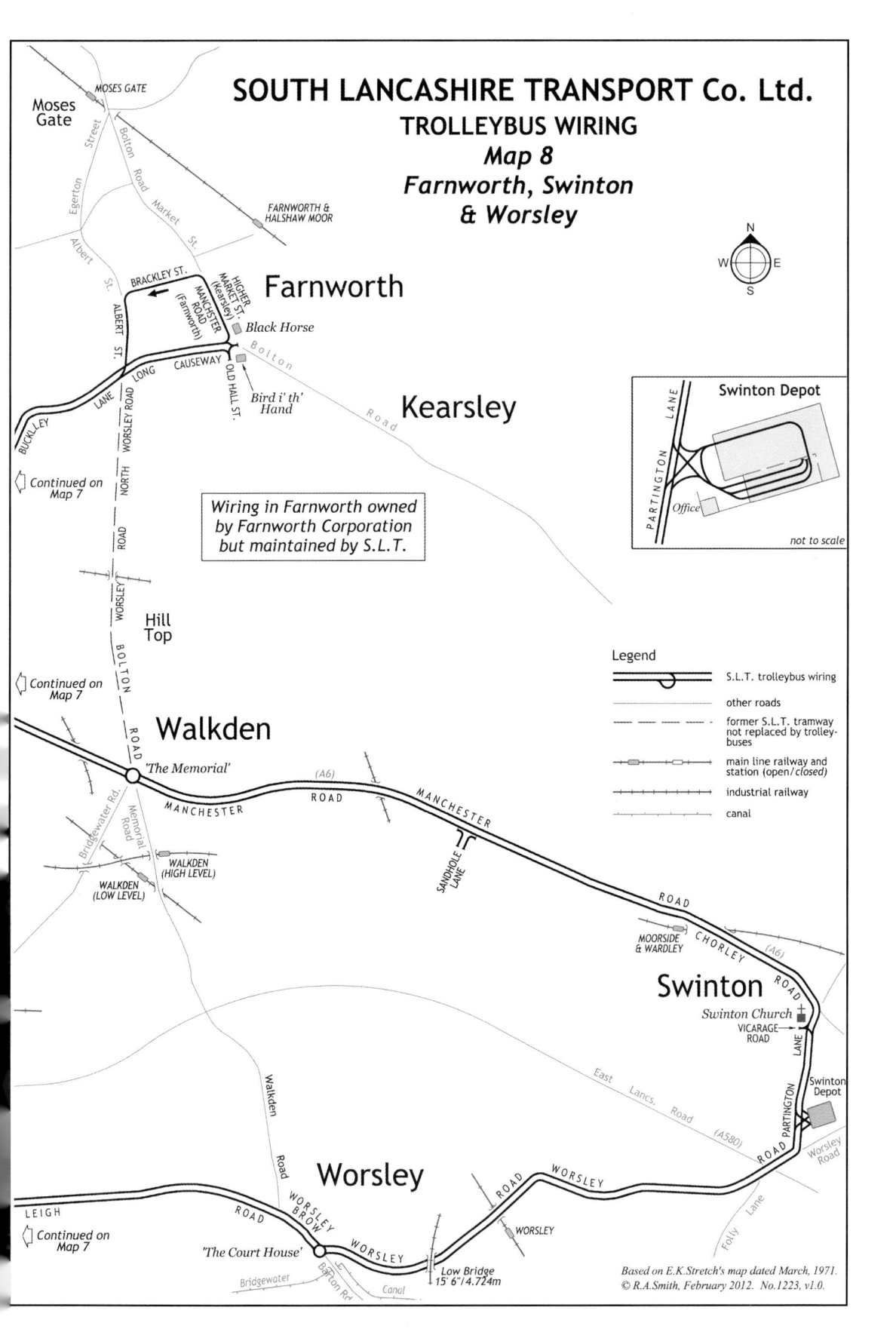

THE ROUTES
THE ATHERTON HUB

1. All the SLT trolleybus routes (except the Bolton local journeys), passed through, or terminated at Atherton. There was a one-way system of wiring around the town centre, the main focal point being the 'Punch Bowl' public house, at the junction of Market Street with Wigan Road and Leigh Road. It is therefore appropriate to start the pictorial journey at this point. Guy trolleybus no 12, with rebuilt front, is about to turn into Wigan Road, with two of the 1938 built Leylands following behind. Note that although the trolleybuses observed a one–way traffic flow, Market Street carried two-way traffic. (Roy Brook)

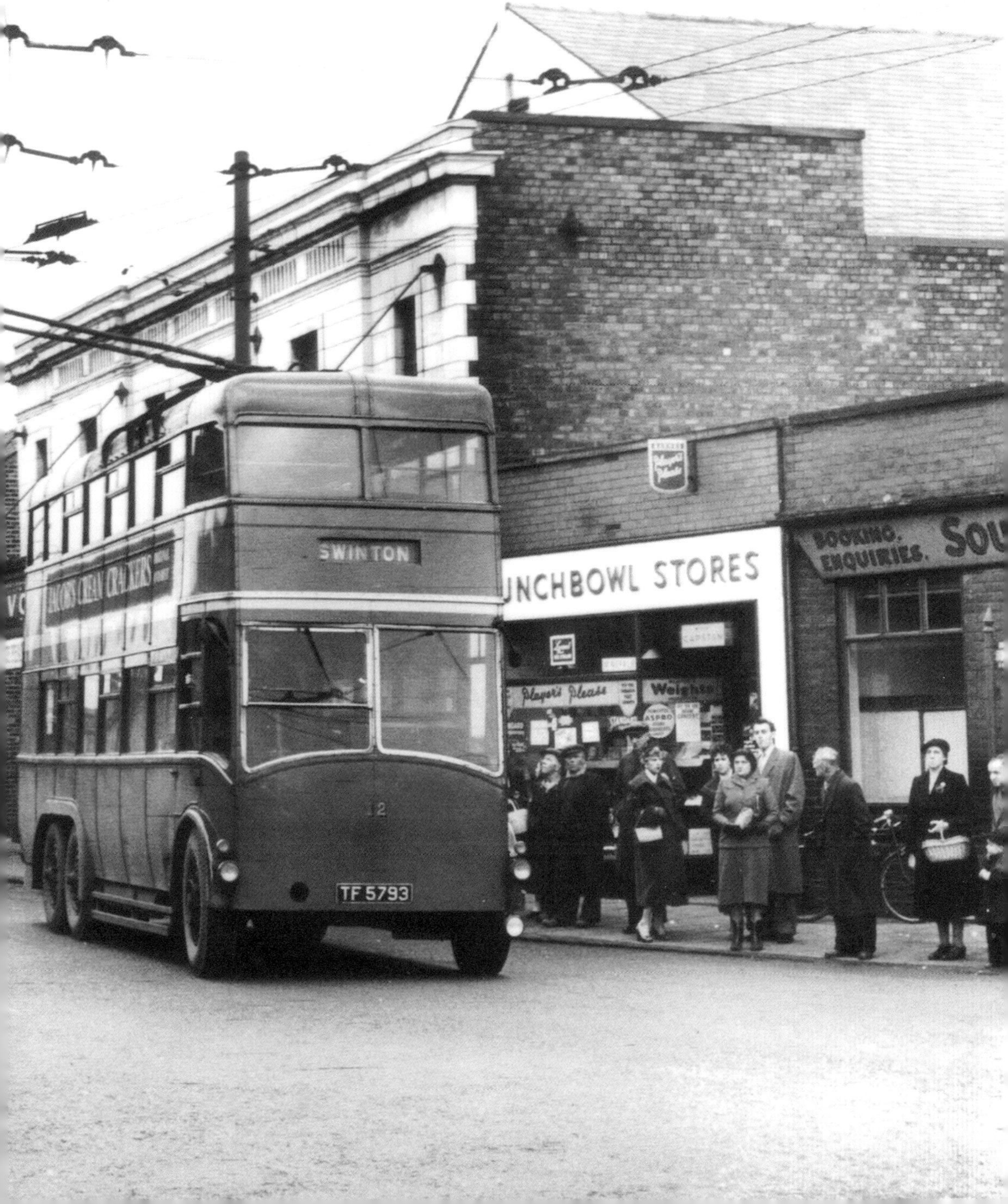
SWINTON
UNCHBOWL STORES
BOOKING. ENQUIRIES.
TF 5793

Still the Best
OZONE
Gentle Action Bleach
HTD 866
HTD 864
SAVOY

A579
BOLTON
A577
MANCHESTER
A579
LEIGH
HALT
BOLTON
VERNONS
DTC 266

← 2. Another busy scene at the 'Punch Bowl' (seen on the left) shows post-war Karrier / Sunbeam no 69 turning into Wigan Road, the conductor having just jumped back onto the platform after pulling the frog handle. Its destination shows 'Bolton', so it must be working Bolton-Atherton short journeys, unlike the similar Karrier behind (no 67) which is working through to Leigh. (H Luff/Online Transport Archive)

← 3. The main stops for the Bolton, and Swinton/Mosley Common services were in Wigan Road. Here, heading for Bolton on a damp day, is Leyland no 59, one of six purchased in 1938. In the far left background can be seen one of the post-war Karrier / Sunbeam vehicles at the Leigh stop outside the SLT enquiry office opposite the 'Punch Bowl'. (Roy Brook)

4. Seen at the Swinton/Mosley Common stop in Wigan Road working a journey on the latter service is no 52, one of the six Leyland TTB type trolleybuses new in 1936/7. (R Marshall)

5. This view at the Swinton / Mosley Common stop shows unrebuilt Guy no 24 in its immediate post-war livery with grey roof and two white bands. In 1955 this vehicle was rebuilt with a new front, being the last trolleybus to receive this modification - see photograph no 61.
(DA Jones)

← 6. The cats-cradle of wiring shown here was at the junction of Wigan Road and Mealhouse Lane. The reversing triangle for the St Helens route terminus is seen on the left, where trolleybuses reversed into Lambeth Street. The wires from Wigan Road into Mealhouse Lane, used by all the other trolleybus services, are in the upper right of view and they passed under the support wires of the triangle. The left turn from the St Helens route into Mealhouse Lane was wired to provide for vehicles being transferred from Platt Bridge depot to Atherton depot. In the opposite direction the wires seen in the left centre were used to gain access to the St Helens route. No facing frog was provided for this latter link, vehicles being required to have their poles transferred manually. Guy six-wheeler no 17 is unloading passengers, having just arrived from St Helens. (Roy Brook)

7. Mealhouse Lane runs parallel with Market Street, and trolleybuses ran along here to the Bolton Road junction. Note the typical Lancashire terraced housing. Post-war Karrier / Sunbeam no 70 makes the turn from Wigan Road, showing the flared lower panels, a distinctive feature of these vehicles. By the time this photograph was taken, the St Helens route wires had been removed. (P Caunt)

8. This is the junction of Bolton Road and Bolton Old Road, a point known as the 'Bacca Shop' (the tobacconist shop on the right). Here the Bolton route and routes towards Swinton parted company. This early post-war view dated February 1948 shows the junction wiring layout and the rear of Guy trolleybus no 17 bound for Bolton in Bolton Road. The inbound wires from Bolton cross into Church Street, leading to Market Street. (Wigan Archive Service, WLCT)

9. Another view of the 'Bacca Shop' junction is seen here, taken ten years after photograph no 8. Leyland trolleybus no 59 is proceeding towards Bolton. The building with the dome in the background is Atherton Town Hall. (Roy Brook)

10. At the junction of Church Street and Market Street, seen in the background to this view, the trolleybuses from Bolton met those from Swinton, and both then ran along Market Street towards the 'Punch Bowl'. Four-wheeler no 44, with modernised front, is seen in Market Street bound for Leigh, having probably come from Mosley Common. Atherton Parish Church dominates the background, and on the right is the 'Jolly Nailor' public house, its name derived from one of the area's oldest industries, nail making. (Roy Brook)

11. There was a useful wiring link in Bag Lane, between Mealhouse Lane and Market Street. This allowed vehicles running from Leigh and terminating at Atherton to turn round. It also enabled vehicles to transfer between Platt Bridge depot on the St Helens route, and Atherton depot. This view shows Guy four-wheeler no 32 turning into Market Street from Bag Lane whilst working Leigh – Atherton journeys. (Roy Brook)

12. The main Leigh stop in Atherton was at the Savoy Cinema, outside the SLT enquiry office and opposite the 'Punch Bowl'. Here, no 63, one of the six wartime 'utility' Karrier vehicles is waiting to depart. It still retains both side and headlights on the front dash panel. Note the blackboards outside the enquiry office, no doubt advertising forthcoming coach excursions. (C Carter)

13. A wider view of the Leigh stop at the Savoy is shown here. A Guy six-wheeler is seen waiting to depart for Leigh in February 1948. On the left is the 'Punch Bowl' and the wiring from Leigh curving round into Wigan Road. (Wigan Archive Service, WLCT)

WEST TO ST HELENS

14. Returning to the Wigan Road/Mealhouse Lane junction, we now look at the Atherton terminus of the St Helens route, worked jointly with St Helens Corporation. Guy trolleybus no 9, in unrebuilt condition apart from the flat dash panel, prepares to reverse. Note that it has pulled across the road and is standing under the wires turning into Mealhouse Lane. The conductor is in position to supervise the reversing movement, and in the distance an LUT Guy motorbus can be seen approaching Atherton. (Roy Brook)

15.   No 8 is seen whilst reversing into Lambeth Street on 2nd May 1954. Note the driver looking back through the half-open cab door. (J Copland)

16.   A view of no 4 in Lambeth Street waiting in the shade to turn back into Wigan Road and return to St Helens. Note the dipped mudguards to the rear wheels, a feature not evident on other photographs of this vehicle (see photograph no 32). The corner shop, with a 'Beech Nut' chewing gum dispenser at the doorway, has a blind across the front window to protect the contents from the sun. (RF Mack, British Trolleybus Society collection)

17. The usual type of St Helens Corporation vehicle latterly used on the service was the ten 1945 Sunbeam Ws with Roe 'utility' lowbridge bodies. They were numbered 105 to 114 (renumbered to 305 to 314 in 1955). No 310 is seen at Lambeth Street in the same position as the SLT vehicle in the previous photograph. St Helens vehicles displayed service no 1 to denote the Atherton route but SLT trolleybuses never used service numbers (although the replacing LUT motorbuses did use the number '1'). Note the covered pavement on the right. (Roy Brook)

18. The route to St Helens was 14 miles long and due to a restrictive bridge near Hindley (removed in 1953), was worked exclusively by lowbridge type vehicles. The SLT vehicles working the route all had to be specifically licensed to work within St Helens Borough. In the 1950s, the service frequency was every 12 minutes, requiring 8 SLT vehicles and 4 from St Helens. Guy no 3, largely unrebuilt, is seen at Atherton, having just arrived from St Helens, and prior to reversing. The 1950s advertising hoardings give a period feel to this view. (C Carter)

19. Typically for the SLT system, the route passed through several mining communities, each with a reversing triangle for peak-hour and special journeys to turn. The first one after leaving Atherton was at Hindley Green, (shown as 'Leigh Road' on destination blinds), where four-wheeler no 43 is seen having just reversed into Leigh Road, beside the Post Office. It is operating to Hindley, the next town towards St Helens, a typical unadvertised 'jigger' working.
(J Fozard)

20. At Hindley, the route turned south west from Atherton Road into Liverpool Road towards Platt Bridge. This late 1930s view shows Guy six-wheeler no 7, which has just made the turn into Liverpool Road. The Hindley reverser was at the end of Atherton Road, at Church Street. No 7 is in original condition, although the SLT monogram, which was placed on the front dash, has been replaced by the fleet number. In the early 1950s this vehicle received an extensive body overhaul which considerably changed its appearance (see photographs 26 and 35). (RB Parr, British Trolleybus Society collection)

21. The vehicles for the St Helens route were housed at Platt Bridge depot, which was situated off Liverpool Road, and accessed via Capp Street. Four-wheeler no 40 is seen in the depot doorway. Note also the Lancashire United motorbuses. (Authors collection)

22. A feature of the route was the unmade road at Templeton Road (Platt Bridge), formerly used by the SLT trams. From Liverpool Road, trolleybuses turned left into Lomax Street, then right, as seen here, into Templeton Road, which then led directly to Warrington Road. Guy six-wheeler no 16, later modified with a complete new front (see photograph 24), is incorrectly showing 'Atherton' in this 1948 view, but is in fact operating towards St Helens. (NN Forbes)

23. Looking in the opposite direction to the previous view, Atherton bound St Helens 'utility' Sunbeam no 309 bounces over the rough surface and former tram tracks of Templeton Road. In wet weather the uneven roadway was converted into a series of large lagoons of water.
(D Lawrence, Photos from the Fifties)

24. South of Platt Bridge is the town of Ashton in Makerfield. The reversing triangle here was at the junction of Gerrard Street and Princess Road, where Guy no 16 is seen on 2nd May 1954. The reverser wiring into Princess Road is in the left background. (J Copland)

25. A nearside view of no 9 standing in Gerrard Street with one of the reverser frogs visible just behind the vehicle. Trolleybuses could turn here from both the Atherton and St Helens directions, and Corporation vehicles used service no 2 for such workings.(J Copland)

26. Between Ashton and Haydock, the route traversed Penny Lane where it passed under a bridge carrying the A580 East Lancashire Road. Although not opened for traffic until 1934, the construction of this bridge was the reason why the first SLT trolleybus operation (in 1930) temporarily terminated at Ashton rather than running through to St Helens. Note that the wiring is suspended in the centre of the bridge to allow extra headroom. Negotiating the structure is Atherton bound no 7, one of two Guy six-wheelers which had extensive body rebuilds in 1953, incorporating rubber mounted windows. (NN Forbes)

➔ 27. The boundary between SLT and St Helens trolleybus operations was at Haydock, 'Rams Head'. Here, the reversing triangle was used by both operators, a regular St Helens service to and from the town centre being designated no 3. It had previously run across the town to Ackers Lane until the closure of the latter route in 1952. The 'Rams Head' dominates this view of SLT no 11 on a journey from St Helens, whilst a St Helens lowbridge utility Sunbeam is using the reverser wiring before returning to St Helens. The SLT vehicle still has a grey roof in this 1954 view. (J Copland)

➔ 28. En route to the terminus in St Helens town centre, the SLT vehicles traversed Cotham Street, passing the Town Hall where four-wheeler no 40 is seen, its destination blind already changed for the return journey. The wiring on the nearside of the vehicle was used by St Helens town services. (Roy Brook)

MAGEE'S ALE
TF 5792

ATHERTON
Homepride SELF-RAISING FLOUR
40
TJ 3329

ATHERTON
LITTLEWOODS
13
TF 5240

PRESCOT 8
IREL COFFEE
FULLY SWEETENED
PURE SUGAR
TJ3328

← 29. The St Helens terminus was in Ormskirk Street at Sefton Place outside Ridings' furniture store. Vehicles reached here after turning left from Cotham Street (in the left background). Elderly, but smart looking no 13 waits before departure in 1954. (J Copland)

← 30. Ormskirk Street was used by other Corporation trolleybus services, including the Prescot and Rainhill circulars, which were operated in the main by post-war Sunbeam and BUT vehicles. In this animated view, SLT four-wheeler no 39 is about to be passed by St Helens BUT no 186 on its way to the Market terminus in Bridge Street. After the St Helens system closed in 1958, the latter vehicle was sold to Bradford, where it ran until 1967. (J Fozard)

31 The Atherton trolleybus service left St Helens town centre via Church Street and Parr Street, joining the inbound wires at Higher Parr Street. This delightful scene, dated about 1950, shows SLT Guy no 9, which has just departed for Atherton, in Church Street where trolleybuses travelled only in the easterly direction. The British Glass Thornycroft lorry is about to turn left into Bridge Street, and the driver's mate is giving a hand signal to this effect. Glass manufacture was, and still is, the principal industry of St Helens. (C Carter)

EAST TO SWINTON

32. Two services used the route from Atherton towards Swinton, these being the Mosley Common service originating from Leigh and the Swinton service, both running every 15 minutes, although the former had a curious 2-3 hour gap in the mid-morning Monday to Friday timetable. The Swinton service ran through beyond Swinton to Farnworth by a very indirect route of over 14 miles, one of the longest trolleybus routes in the country. Shortly after passing the 'Bacca Shop', trolleybuses bound for Swinton turned right into High Street, to run down to Tyldesley Road, where they joined the inbound route. Guy six-wheeler no 4 is seen in High Street on the last Saturday of trolleybus operation, 29th August 1958. By this time it was the only trolleybus in largely un-rebuilt condition to remain in use. (J Kaye)

LEIGH — ATHERTON — TYLDESLEY — MOSLEY COMMON — Trolley Bus Service

MONDAY TO FRIDAY		am	am	am	am	am	am	am	am	am	am	am	am	am	am	am
Leigh, Spinning Jenny Street	dep.	...	...	...	5 40	5 55	...	...	...	...	...	7 25	7 40	7 55	8 10	8 25	8 40
Atherton, Depot	,,	4 36	5 18	5 33	5 48	6 3	...	...	7 3	7 18	7 33	7 48	8 3	8 18	8 33	8 48
Atherton, Punch Bowl	,,	4 40	5 22	5 37	5 52	6 7	6 22	6 37	6 52	7 7	7 22	7 37	7 52	8 7	8 22	8 37	8 52
Tyldesley, Co-op. Stores	,,	4 50	5 32	5 47	6 2	6 17	6 32	6 47	7 2	7 17	7 32	7 47	8 2	8 17	8 32	8 47	9 2
Mosley Common	arr.	5 0	5 42	5 57	6 12	6 27	6 42	6 57	7 12	7 27	7 42	7 57	8 12	8 27	8 42	8 57	...

		am	am	am		pm	pm	pm	pm		pm	pm	SATURDAY			
Leigh, Spinning Jenny Street	dep.	...	...	1155	and	7 55	...	...	...	and	...	...	am	am	am	am
Atherton, Depot	,,	1133	1148	12 3	every	8 3	...	...	...	every	...	...	9 33	9 48	10 3	1018
Atherton, Punch Bowl	,,	1137	1152	12 7	15 mins.	8 7	8 22	8 37	8 52	15 mins.	1052	11 7	9 37	9 52	10 7	1022
Tyldesley, Co-op. Stores	,,	1147	12 2	1217	until	8 17	8 32	8 47	9 2	until	11 2	1117	9 47	10 2	1017	1032
Mosley Common	arr.	1157	1212	1227		8 27	8 42	8 57	9 12		1112	...	9 57	1012	1027	1042

SATURDAY, continued		am	am		pm	pm	pm	SUNDAY					pm		pm	pm	pm
Leigh, Spinning Jenny Street	dep.	...	1040	and	1048	1055	11 5	...	...	...	...	...	2 40	and	1040	1055	11 5
Atherton, Depot	,,	1033	1048	every	1048	11 3	1113	1 33	1 48	2 3	2 18	2 33	2 48	every	1048	11 3	1113
Atherton, Punch Bowl	,,	1037	1052	15	1052	11 7	1117	1 37	1 52	2 7	2 22	2 37	2 52	15	1052	11 7	1117
Tyldesley, Co-op. Stores	,,	1047	11 2	mins.	11 2	1117	...	1 47	2 2	2 17	2 32	2 47	3 2	mins.	11 2	1117	...
Mosley Common	arr.	1057	1112	until	1112	...	...	1 57	2 12	2 27	2 42	2 57	3 12	until	1112	...	...

MONDAY to FRIDAY		am	am	am	am	am	am	am	am	am	am	am	am	am	am	am
Mosley Common	dep.	5 0	5 43	5 58	6 13	6 28	6 43	6 58	7 13	7 28	7 43	7 58	8 13	8 28	8 43	...	8 58
Tyldesley, Market	,,	5 10	5 53	6 8	6 23	6 38	6 53	7 8	7 23	7 38	7 53	8 8	8 23	8 38	8 53	9 3	9 8
Atherton, Punch Bowl	,,	5 20	6 3	6 18	6 33	6 48	7 3	7 18	7 33	7 48	8 3	8 18	8 33	8 48	9 3	9 13	9 18
Atherton, Depot	,,	5 24	...	...	...	...	7 7	7 22	7 37	7 52	8 7	8 22	8 37	8 52	9 7	9 17	9 22
Leigh, Spinning Jenny Street	arr.	5 32	...	...	...	...	7 15	7 30	7 45	8 0	8 15	8 30	8 45	9 0	...	...	...

		am	am	pm		pm	pm	pm	pm		pm	pm	pm			
Mosley Common	dep.	1158	1213	1228	and	7 13	7 28	7 43	7 58	and	1058	...	1113			
Tyldesley, Market	,,	12 8	1223	1238	every	7 23	7 38	7 53	8 8	every	11 8	1118	1123			
Atherton, Punch Bowl	,,	1218	1233	1248	15 mins.	7 33	7 48	8 3	8 18	15 mins.	1118	1128	1133			
Atherton, Depot	,,	1222	1237	1252	until	7 37	7 52	8 7	...	until	1122	1132	1137			
Leigh, Spinning Jenny Street	arr.	1230	1245	1 0		7 45	...	...	...		...	...	...			

SATURDAY		am	am	am	am		pm	pm	pm	pm	pm					
Mosley Common	dep.	9 58	1013	1028	1043	and	1028	1043	1058	...	1113					
Tyldesley, Market	,,	10 8	1023	1038	1053	every	1038	1053	11 8	1118	1123					
Atherton, Punch Bowl	,,	1018	1033	1048	11 3	15 mins.	1048	11 3	1118	1128	1133					
Atherton, Depot	,,	1022	1037	1052	11 7	until	1052	11 7	1122	1132	1137					
Leigh, Spinning Jenny Street	arr.	1030	1045	11 0	1115		11 0	...	...	...	...					

SUNDAY		pm	pm	pm			pm	pm	pm	pm	pm					
Mosley Common	dep.	1 58	2 13	2 28	and		1028	1043	1058	...	1113					
Tyldesley, Market	,,	2 8	2 23	2 38	every		1038	1053	11 8	1118	1123					
Atherton, Punch Bowl	,,	2 18	2 33	2 48	15 mins.		1048	11 3	1118	1128	1133					
Atherton, Depot	,,	2 22	2 37	2 52	until		1052	11 7	1122	1132	1137					
Leigh, Spinning Jenny Street	arr.	2 30	2 45	3 0			11 0	...	...	...	...					

33. A feature of the SLT trolleybus operation was the process for turning trolleybuses when roads were closed for religious processions, a frequent event in this area of Lancashire. Two pairs of bamboo poles connected by insulated cables were used, one pair being attached to the vehicle's trolleyheads and the other to the overhead. This allowed the trolleybuses sufficient manoeuvring room to execute a three point turn in the absence of any overhead wiring. In this view on Tyldesley Road, Atherton, it would appear that the process has almost been completed and the trolley booms of Guy no 13 will be placed on the overhead to allow it to return towards Swinton.(EK Stretch)

Sunfresh
WINTON
42

SUNSHINE BREAKFAST!
CORN FLAKES
ALL LEADING MAKES OF TELEVISION
COMMERCIAL MODELS AVAILABLE IMMEDIATE DELIVERY
RIDINGS
TF 2078

← 34. The first major settlement east of Atherton was Tyldesley, where, as at Atherton, trolleybuses operated a one way system around the central streets. West bound vehicles used Elliott Street, whereas eastbound they used Shuttle Street, then Milk Street to join the westbound wires at the eastern end of Elliott Street. Swinton bound four-wheeler no 42 is seen in Milk Street, about to turn into Elliot Street at the end of the one-way section. Note that there was a wiring link here to allow vehicles to turn back towards Atherton, and the facing frog for this can be seen in the top centre of this view. (P Mitchell)

← 35. On the westbound one-way section, rebuilt no 7 is seen in Elliott Street at Astley Street. The extent of the rebuild (already noted) is evident. (Author's collection)

36. Between Tyldesley and Mosley Common, the route traversed Sale Lane, where one of the pair of 1937 built Leylands, no 53 is seen on the Mosley Common to Leigh through service. (P Mitchell)

37. Having come along Mosley Common Road from Parr Brow, Guy no 1 turns to run along Sale Lane towards Tyldesley. This vehicle was extensively rebuilt in 1953. (P Mitchell)

38. This scene is at Mosley Common, and four-wheeler no 42 has just departed from the terminus of the service to Leigh, which was the only SLT all day service to be regularly operated by both high and lowbridge vehicles. No 42 was one of only two of the four-wheel Guys which were modernised with deep side panelling (the other being no 44). (P Mitchell)

39. Trolleybuses terminating at Mosley Common turned using a reversing triangle at Bridgewater Road. 'Utility' Karrier no 64 is seen here having reversed, and before turning back onto Mosley Common Road. The Mosley Common colliery, which provided considerable passenger traffic for the trolleybuses, is in the right background. (P Mitchell)

40. A short distance east of Mosley Common, the Swinton route crossed the East Lancashire Road. Well filled Guy no 28 is seen here coming from the Boothstown direction towards Atherton. (Roy Brook)

41. In Boothstown proper, Guy four-wheeler no 42 is seen in Chaddock Lane, amidst the backdrop of a small Lancashire industrial town. Retreating into the distance is another trolleybus, about to be passed by a Salford City Transport bus on the joint LUT/Salford service 26 to Leigh. (Roy Brook)

42. The short working turning provision at Boothstown was in Leigh Road at Cooper Street. This consisted of two detached pairs of wires in Cooper Street itself (on the right, beside the advertising hoarding). To turn using power meant three trolley pole changes for the crew, but the turn could be made more easily using gravity to reverse into Cooper Street and drive out. Despite the awkwardness of the provision, there were regular twice daily turns at this point. On the right of this view, Guy four-wheeler no 41 has just completed the turn and its poles will be placed on the wires after six-wheeler no 18 has passed, The Cooper Street wires are tied off to the traction pole on the left. (Roy Brook)

43. Heading east along Leigh Road from Boothstown towards Worsley, the surroundings of the route became more genteel, serving pre-war housing. Atherton bound Guy four-wheeler no 35, one of this type which retained its original bulbous front dash, is seen setting down passengers near Ellenbrook Road. The restrictive ex-tramway overhead construction on this section would not allow trolleybuses to pull fully into the kerb at stops. (Roy Brook)

44. Further along Leigh Road were detached houses of the more well-to-do (including the General Manager of SLT). This part of the route was one of the rural sections of the system, as demonstrated in this view of Atherton bound four-wheeler no 32. The detached housing is to the left, with green fields on the right. (J S King)

45. Climbing from the Walkden Road / Worsley Brow junction is Guy six-wheeler no 20. The spire of St Mark's Church Worsley is in the background. (J S King)

46.   After a short run along Worsley Brow, trolleybuses reached Worsley Court House junction, where there was a full circle of overhead to allow short working from either the Atherton or Swinton direction. It was here that trolleybuses working through to Farnworth changed their destination from 'Swinton' to 'Farnworth'. No 19 is seen here, ready to depart for Farnworth. This vehicle, along with no 2, was one of only two Guy six-wheelers that retained most of their original features, including the bulbous dash panel. The lower deck staircase window has been replaced by an inset panel. (DF Parker)

47.   Guy no 15 catches the sun as it arrives at Worsley Court House from Worsley Road. The circle wiring is just visible above the vehicle. (Travel Lens Photographic)

48.   Shortly beyond The Court House junction, trolleybuses passed over the famous canal entrance to the Duke of Bridgewater's mines. The parapet of the bridge is seen on the left, as Guy six-wheeler no 4 approaches Mill Brow. In the background, standing next to the attractive half-timbered building, is the white 3-storey head office of the Bridgewater Estates. (JS King)

Leaflet No. 538

Leyland

THE LEYLAND-G·E·C·
LOW-FLOOR
TROLLEY BUS
PATENTS APPLIED FOR

Leyland Motors Ltd

Printed in England

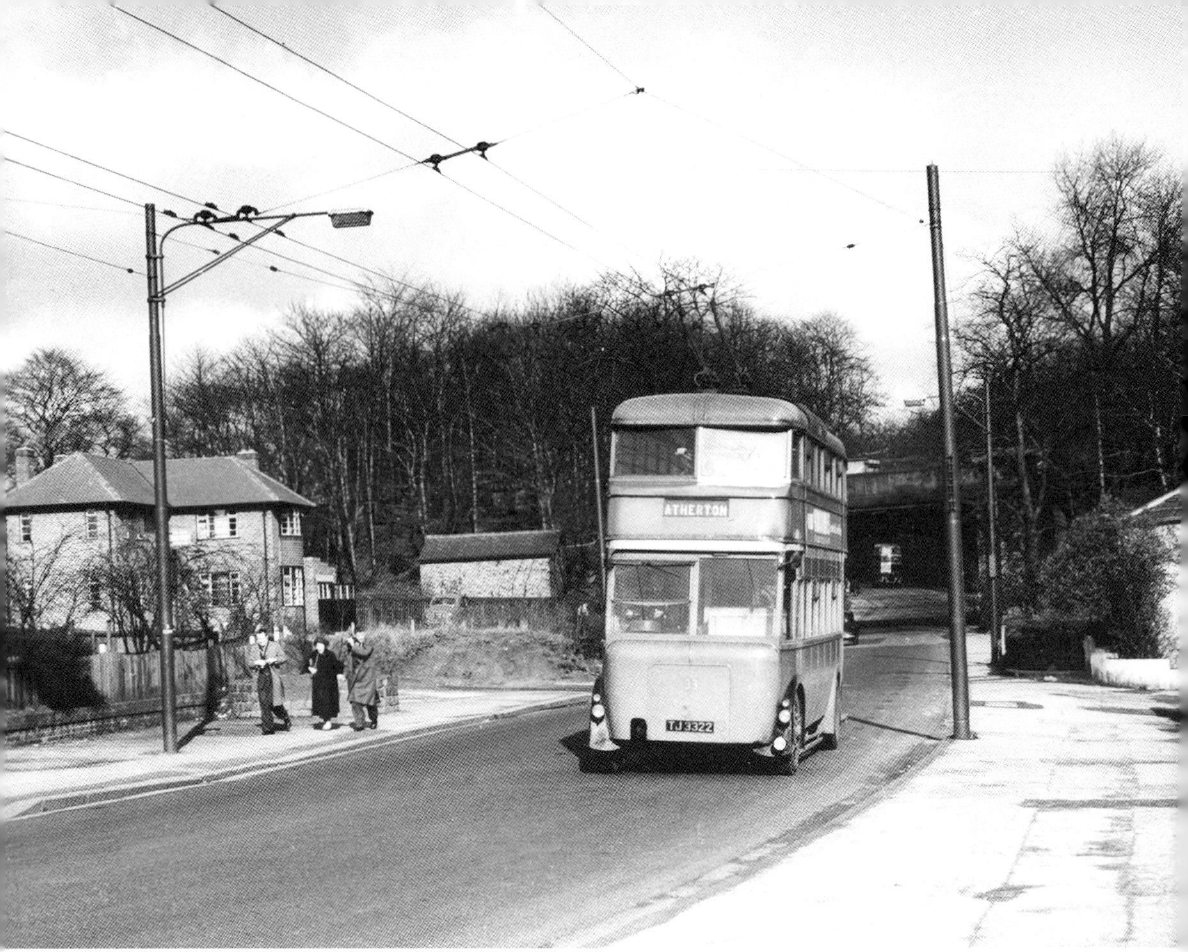
ATHERTON
TJ 3322

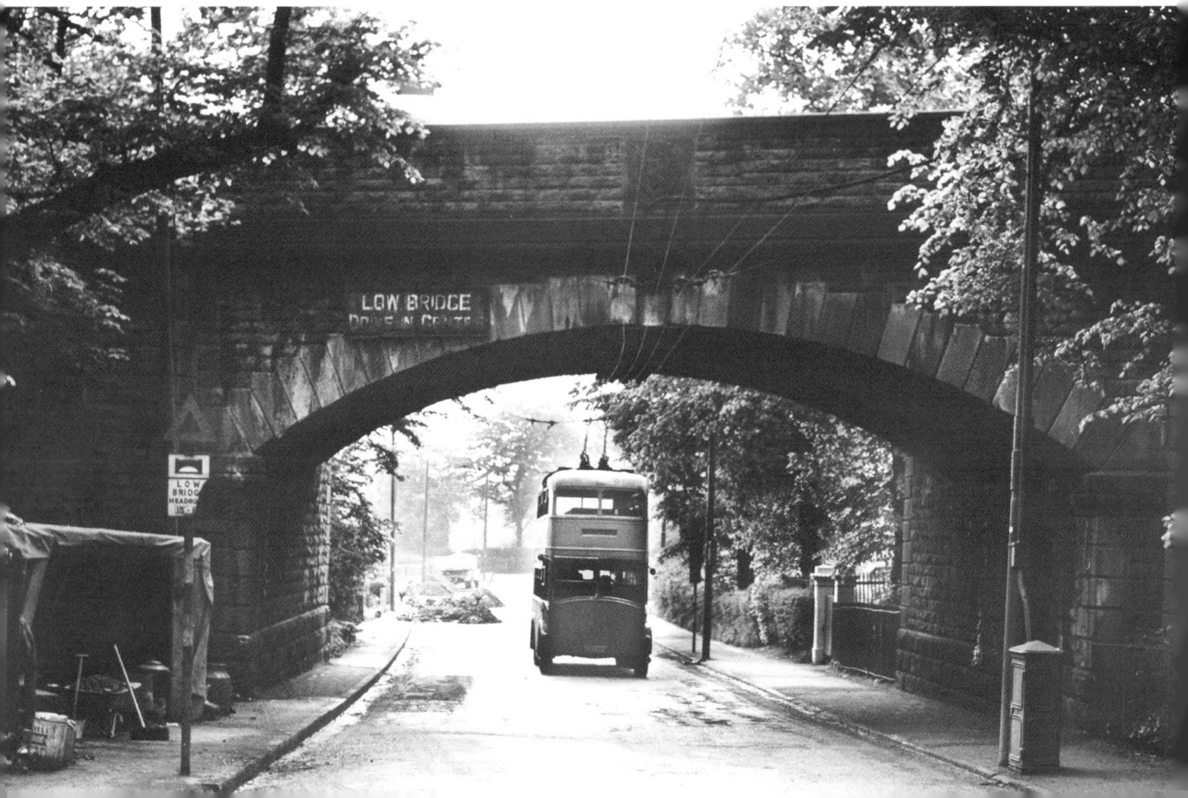
LOW BRIDGE

← 49. Guy 4-wheeler no 33 passes through the pleasant surroundings of Worsley Green on a journey to Atherton. The bridge just visible in the background is described in the next photograph. (JS King)

← 50. The bridge on Worsley Road at Worsley Green carried a colliery railway and was one of two on the Farnworth route which meant that, for most of the life of the system, only lowbridge vehicles could work east of Worsley. This rule was relaxed in the last year or so of operation, when it was found that the highbridge vehicles could just pass under these bridges. Lowbridge Guy six-wheeler no 23 negotiates the bridge on a journey towards Swinton. Note how the overhead wires are positioned very close together underneath the centre of the arch. (Roy Brook)

51. Having negotiated the railway bridge, Guy six-wheeler no 11 heads through the trees towards Swinton and Farnworth. Although not clear due to the bare branches, the traction pole on the right does not have a span wire attached to it because of decay. The wire is actually secured to the tree! (JS King)

ATHERTON
TF 5806
WORSLEY
STATION
PARK YOUR
CAR HERE

JACOB'S
Cream Crackers
TF 2072

← 52. Further along Worsley Road was Worsley railway station, where six-wheeler no 28, bound for Atherton, is seen in this pleasant rural setting. The station was closed in 1969. (Roy Brook)

← 53. A study of much rebuilt trolleybus no 1 standing in the sunshine at the Co-operative store on Worsley Road at Moorside Road. (J Fozard)

54. Nearing Swinton, trolleybuses crossed the East Lancashire Road again, and six-wheeler no 20 is seen, proceeding from Swinton towards Worsley. (Roy Brook)

ATHERTON—SWINTON : SWINTON—WALKDEN : WALKDEN—LITTLE HULTON AND FARNWORTH Sections (Trackless Trolley 'Buses)

MONDAY TO FRIDAY

		am	am	am	am	am	am	am	am	am		pm	pm	pm	pm	pm
Atherton, Punch Bowl	dep.	...	...	...	...	...	5 0	5 15	5 30	5 45		10 0	1015	1030	1045	11 0
Tyldesley, Co-op. Stores	,,	...	...	...	...	...	5 10	5 25	5 40	5 55		1010	1025	1040	1055	1110
Mosley Common	,,	...	...	...	...	...	5 20	5 35	5 50	6 5		1020	1035	1050	11 5	1120
Boothstown, Greyhound	,,	...	...	...	...	...	5 23	5 38	5 53	6 8	and	1023	1038	1053	11 8	1123
Worsley, Court House	,,	...	...	...	...	5 19	5 30	5 45	6 0	6 15	every	1030	1045	11 0	1115	1130
Swinton, Church	arr.	...	...	...	...	5 30	5 41	5 56	6 11	6 26	15 mins.	1041	1056	1111	1126	1141
Swinton, Church	dep.	4 30	4 45	5 0	5 15	5 30	5 45	6 0	6 15	6 30	until	1045	11 0	...	...	...
Walkden, Memorial	,,	4 42	4 57	5 12	5 27	5 42	5 57	6 12	6 27	6 42		1057	1112	...	...	...
Cleggs Lane	,,	4 47	5 2	5 17	5 32	5 47	6 2	6 17	6 32	6 47		11 2	...	...	...	...
Farnworth, Brackley Street	arr.	4 57	5 12	5 27	5 42	5 57	6 12	6 27	6 42	6 57		1112	...	...	...	...

		am	am	am	am	am	am		pm	pm	pm	pm	pm
Farnworth, Brackley Street	dep.	...	...	5 0	5 15	5 30	5 45		1030	1045	11 0	1115	
Cleggs Lane	,,	...	...	5 9	5 24	5 39	5 54		1039	1054	...	11 9	1124
Walkden, Memorial	,,	...	...	5 14	5 29	5 44	5 59		1044	1059	1112	1114	1129
Swinton, Church	arr.	...	...	5 26	5 41	5 56	6 11	and	1056	1111	1124	1126	1141
Swinton, Church	dep.	4 59	5 14	5 29	5 44	5 59	6 14	every	1059	...	...	...	...
Worsley, Court House	,,	5 10	5 25	5 40	5 55	6 10	6 25	15 mins.	1110	...	...	...	...
Boothstown, Greyhound	,,	5 17	5 32	5 47	6 2	6 17	6 32	until	1117	...	...	...	...
Mosley Common	,,	5 20	5 35	5 50	6 5	6 20	6 35		1120	...	...	...	...
Tyldesley, Market	,,	5 30	5 45	6 0	6 15	6 30	6 45		1130	...	...	...	...
Atherton, Punch Bowl	arr.	5 40	5 55	6 10	6 25	6 40	6 55		1140	...	...	...	...

The above service will be augmented between Swinton and Farnworth as follows :—

Swinton to Farnworth. Mon. to Fri.—4-38 a.m., 5-8 a.m. and every 15 mins. until 8-23 a.m. then 3-8 p.m. and every 15 mins. until 6-53 p.m.

Farnworth to Swinton. Mon. to Fri.—5-8 a.m., 5-38 a.m. and every 15 mins. until 8-53 a.m. then 3-38 p.m. and every 15 mins. until 7-23 p.m.

Railway Stations on or near the route

Tyldesley, Stanley Street for Tyldesley Station
Worsley Station. Moorside and Wardley Station.

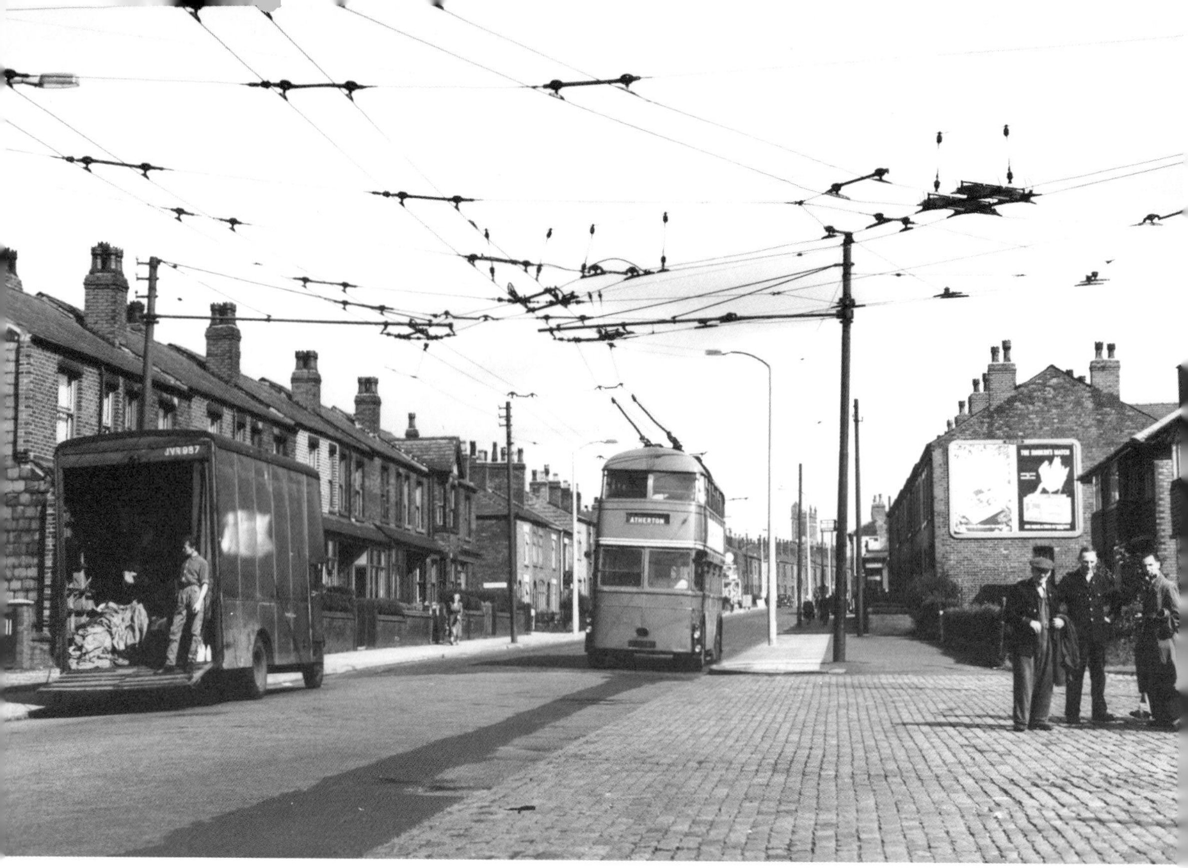
JVR 957
ATHERTON

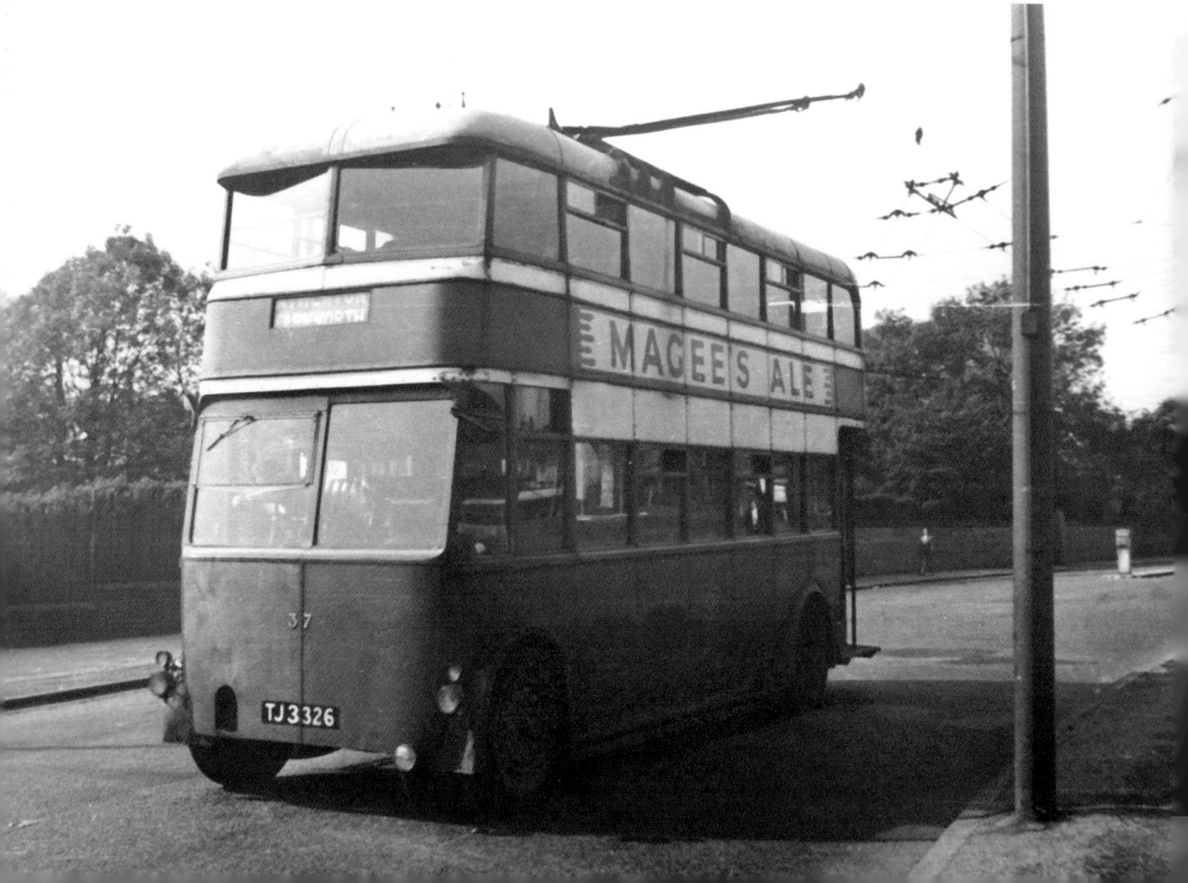
MAGEE'S ALE
37
TJ3326

← 55. Beyond the East Lancashire Road crossing, trolleybuses turned sharp left from Worsley Road into Partington Lane, where the Swinton depot was situated. This view dates from the final month of the system, August 1958, during the period when highbridge trolleybuses were seen on this route, hence the presence of Leyland no 55 standing in Partington Lane outside the depot. (Roy Brook)

← 56. At Swinton Church, there was a reversing triangle at Vicarage Road. This was used by the local service running between Swinton and Farnworth which, combined with the through Atherton service, provided a 7½ minute frequency. Four-wheeler no 37 is seen about to reverse across Partington Lane into Vicarage Road on such a local service working. (DF Parker)

57. Six-wheeler no 20 is seen here in the apex of the reversing triangle at Swinton Church. (J Fozard)

ATHERTON
WOODBINE
27
TF 5806

Enjoy SWALES STOUT
HALFWAY HOUSE
FARNWORTH
AUSTIN
44

← 58. Guy six-wheeler no 27 departs for Atherton on 30th June 1958. In the right background is a green Salford City Transport Daimler bus. At this point Partington Lane had a short section with a paved central strip, as seen here. (J Copland, Colin Wright collection)

← 59. Swinton Church was a major point on the Farnworth route, any through passengers having to re-book here. Four-wheel Guy no 44 stands at the main Atherton bound stop. (Roy Brook)

60. This rather bleak scene at Swinton Church shows four-wheeler no 36 waiting to depart for Atherton. The long corrugated iron shelter looks even more uninviting in the snow. (DF Parker)

SWINTON TO FARNWORTH

61. Towards Farnworth, the route turned sharp left at the 'Bull's Head' onto the A6 Chorley Road. Guy six-wheeler no 24, the last trolleybus to be modernised, waits in Chorley Road at the Swinton Church timing point with the 'Bull's Head' and the road junction in the background. (P Mitchell)

62. Beyond Swinton, the route proceeded along the A6, Manchester Road, passing through open rural scenery. Mid-way to Walkden, at Sandhole Lane near the colliery, there was a detached reverser triangle similar to the arrangement at Boothstown. In this view, Guy six-wheeler no 10 has reached the housing on the approach to Walkden. (P Mitchell)

63. The 'Stocks Hotel', at Walkden is situated just east of the Walkden Memorial (Monument) road junction. Here, Leyland no 58 pauses at the stop before continuing to Swinton and Atherton. These highbridge vehicles appeared on the route only in the last 18 months or so of trolleybus operation, following successful trials negotiating the low bridges at Worsley and Cleggs Lane. (J Fozard)

64. At Walkden Memorial there was a full circle of trolleybus wiring to allow vehicles to turn from either the Swinton or Farnworth direction. Standing in Manchester Road West, Walkden, on 2nd April 1958, just beyond the Memorial, is much rebuilt no 1 with its poles lowered, having possibly suffered a breakdown. Note the inspectors' cabin with power fed from the overhead wires. (PJ Thompson)

➔ 65. The route continued westwards along Manchester Road East (A6) towards Little Hulton. Heavily rebuilt no 7 is seen approaching Little Hulton itself, near Bridgewater Street. (P Mitchell)

➔ 66. At Little Hulton Co-operative store, the route left the A6 road and turned right into Cleggs Lane, towards Farnworth. Along here the overhead wiring had not been modernised, and remained suspended using the old tramway bracket arms. This caused problems for Swinton bound vehicles which could not pull into the kerb at stops. Here passengers have to alight into the road from six-wheeler no 28 at Edward Street. (Roy Brook)

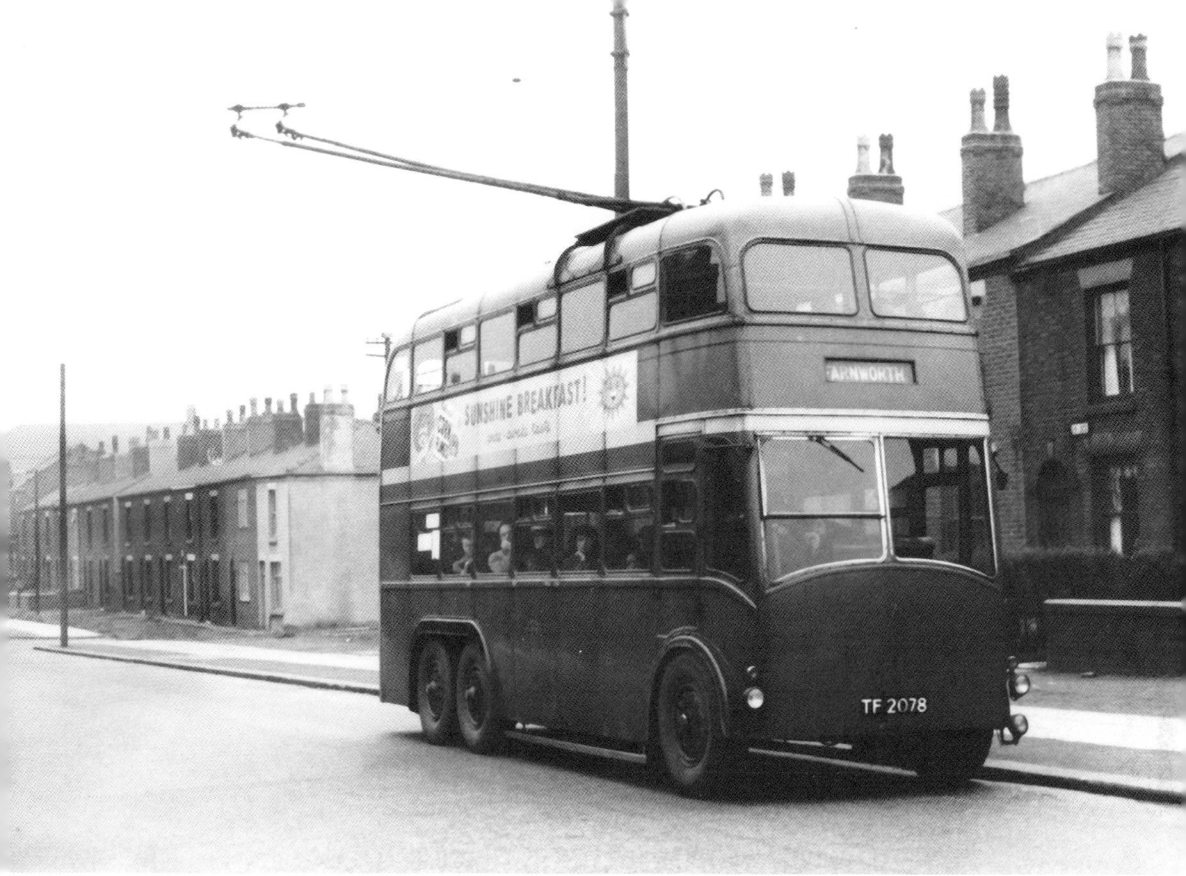
SUNSHINE BREAKFAST!
FARNWORTH
TF 2078

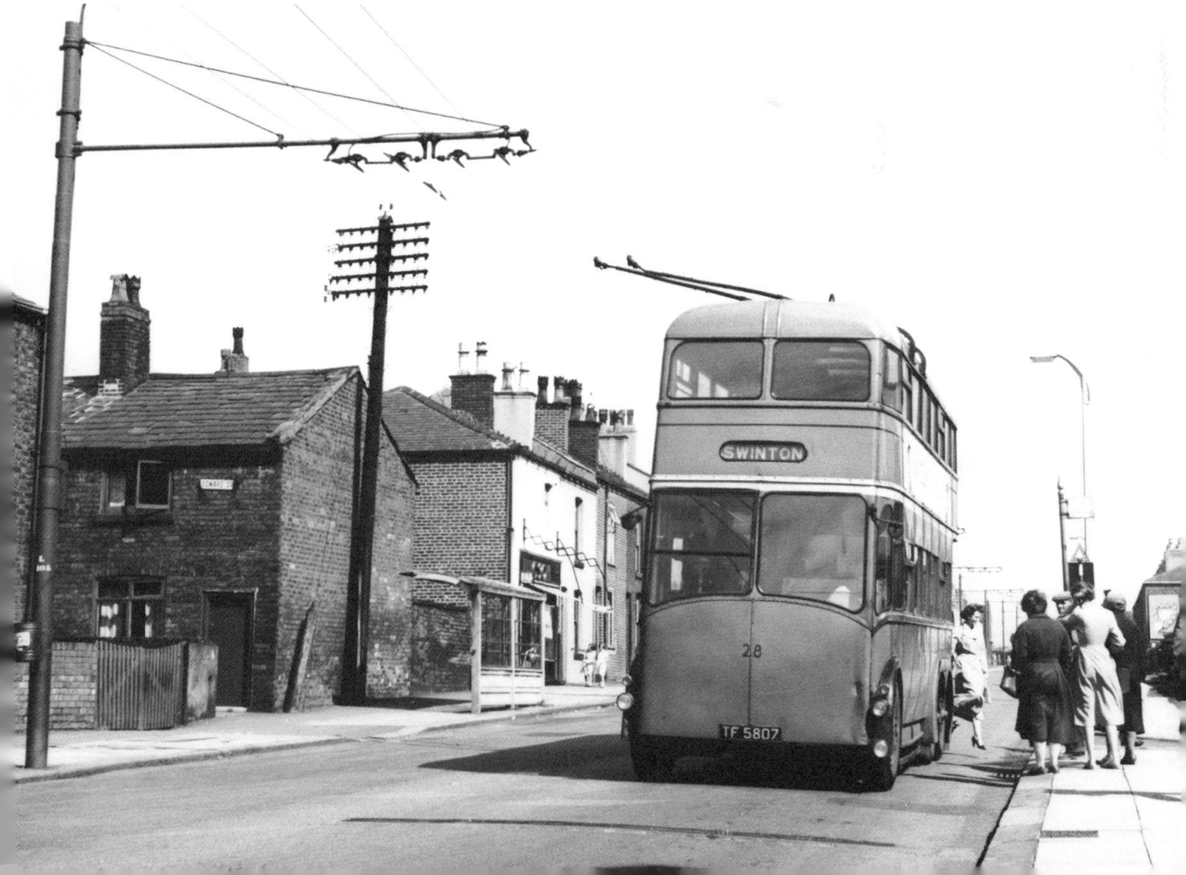
SWINTON
28
TF 5807

67. Further along Cleggs Lane towards Farnworth was this low mineral railway overbridge. Here the wires were positioned towards the kerb to allow maximum headroom for the vehicles, before reverting to the bracket arm suspension which can just be seen beyond the bridge. No 27 proceeds towards Little Hulton. (P Mitchell)

→ 68. From Cleggs Lane, the route joined Buckley Lane for the run into Farnworth town centre. The terminal arrangement for trolleybuses was by means of a long one way 'round the houses' loop, a provision which was introduced in 1936. The original terminus was at the junction of Longcauseway and Manchester Road, where there was a triangular reverser, this being retained for use a few days per year when the main streets of Farnworth were closed for events. This view at Longcauseway dates from 1938, and shows four-wheeler Guy no 38 dropping passengers before turning left into Manchester Road. The vehicle is in original condition, with half-drop windows, stencil destination indicator and the Guy badge on the cab door. (Authors collection)

→ 69. The Farnworth reverser is shown in this view of no 42 turning into Manchester Road on 2nd April 1958. The awkwardness of the arrangement is evident, trolleybuses having to cross the road to a point beyond the 'Bird I'th Hand' public house before reversing into Old Hall Street, and this was one of the reasons why the turning loop was introduced in 1936. Nevertheless, the reverser was retained for emergency use. Note the typical SLT method of wiring construction, using mismatched parts. (PJ Thompson)

SWINTON
TJ 3327
HIPPODROME
WOMEN
MEN MARRY
DOUBLE
WEDDING

MAGEE'S ALE
BOYDELLS

70. Until 1944, the one way trolleybus loop in Manchester Road was shared with the Bolton trams on their Farnworth ('F') service, which terminated at the 'Black Horse'. The tram wires and tracks from Moses Gate to Farnworth were maintained by SLT. This commercial postcard dating from just before the war shows a Bolton tram which has just reversed at the 'Black Horse' (seen on the right), with the one-way trolleybus overhead evident. From here trolleybuses turned left into Brackley Street to reach the Farnworth terminus. (Author's collection)

➔ 71. This is the Brackley Street terminus at Farnworth showing no 29 outside the Co-operative pharmacy store. It is in the overall red livery with grey roof and large shaded fleet numbers. (RF Mack, British Trolleybus Society collection)

➔ 72. Whilst passengers board at the rear, the driver of six-wheeler no 6 proudly stands by his vehicle at Brackley Street terminus before departing on a journey to Swinton only. (Roy Brook)

T for TUROG TUROG for T
THERTON
29
TF 5808

SWINTON
TF2077
BUS STOP

73. Further along Brackley Street, no 18 has just commenced its long journey to Atherton. Note that 'Atherton' was shown all the way from Farnworth, unlike the arrangement for the opposite direction where 'Farnworth' was shown only from Worsley onwards. (P Mitchell)

74. From Brackley Street, the one-way loop turned into Albert Road, and then joined the inbound wires at its junction with Buckley Lane and Longcauseway. There was another Bolton tram route which ran until 1944 in Farnworth along Albert Road on SLT maintained tracks. This was route 'G' which crossed Longcauseway and ran to Walkden. This wartime view shows Bolton tram 330 crossing Longcauseway from Albert Road on a journey to Walkden and passing under the trolleybus wires in Longcauseway. The wires on the left form the start of the one-way loop, whilst those on the right are the return wires from the emergency reverser. The trolleybus wires from Albert Road, at the end of the one-way section join the wires from the reverser by the trailing frog just visible immediately above the centre of the tramcar's roof. (AB Cross)

SOUTH TO LEIGH

75. The Atherton to Leigh route, at 2⅓ miles, was the shortest of the SLT trolleybus sections. It was also the busiest, the Leigh to Bolton service being every 8 ½ minutes, and the Leigh to Mosley Common service being every 15, making a total of eleven trolleybuses per hour. With the 'Punch Bowl' junction visible in the far background, 'utility' Karrier no 62, being overtaken by a motorcycle, comes along Leigh Road towards Howe Bridge. On the left is an example of an SLT trolleybus stop sign, which has black lettering on a yellow background. (JS King)

76. Karrier / Sunbeam MS2 no 66 is passing Atherton Cenotaph on Leigh Road. Hamilton Street is on the right. (J Kaye)

→ 77. This railway bridge was at Howe Bridge railway station, where Karrier / Sunbeam no 71 is seen en route to Leigh. The structure was replaced by a new bridge in 1957. (J Fozard)

LEIGH—ATHERTON—FOUR LANE ENDS—BOLTON
Trolley Vehicle Service

SATURDAY

		am	am	am	am	am	am	am	am	am	am	am	am	am	am	am
Leigh, Spinning Jenny Street	dep.	...	...	...	...	...	5 26	...	...	...	5 52	...	6 9	...	6 26	6 44
Atherton, Depot	,,	4 34	4 43	4 52	5 9	5 26	5 34	5 43	5 52	6 0	6 9	6 17	6 26	6 34	6 43	6 52
Atherton, Punch Bowl	,,	4 38	4 47	4 56	5 13	5 30	5 38	5 47	5 56	6 4	6 13	6 21	6 30	6 38	6 47	6 56
Four Lane Ends	,,	4 50	4 59	5 8	5 25	5 42	5 50	5 59	6 8	6 16	6 25	6 33	6 42	6 50	6 59	7 8
Bolton, Howell Croft	arr.	5 6	...	5 24	5 41	5 58	6 6	6 15	6 24	6 32	6 41	6 49	6 58	7 6	7 15	7 24

		am				pm	pm	pm	pm	pm	pm	pm	pm	pm
Leigh, Spinning Jenny Street	dep.	6 52				1018	1026	1035	1044	1052	1055	11 3	1111	1120
Atherton, Depot	,,	7 0		and		1026	1034	1043	1052	11 0	11 3	1111	1119	1128
Atherton, Punch Bowl	,,	7 4		every		1030	1038	1047	1056	11 4	11 7	1115	1123	1132
Four Lane Ends	,,	7 16		8½ minutes		1042	1050	1059	11 8	1116	1119	...	...	...
Bolton, Howell Croft	arr.	7 32		until		1058	11 6	1115	...	...	...	...	...	...

		am	am	am	am	am			pm	pm	pm	pm		pm	pm
Bolton, Howell Croft	dep.	...	5 6	5 24	5 41	5 58		and	1032	1041	1049	...		1058	...
Four Lane Ends	,,	5 0	5 20	5 38	5 55	6 12		every	1046	1055	11 3	...		11 9	1112
Atherton, Punch Bowl	,,	5 11	5 31	5 49	6 6	6 23		8½ minutes	1057	11 6	1114	1117		1120	1123	1125
Atherton, Depot	,,	5 15	5 35	5 53	6 10	6 27		until	11 1	1110	1118	1121		1124	1127	1129
Leigh, Spinning Jenny Street	arr.	5 23	5 43	6 1	6 18	6 35			11 9	1118	...	...		...	...	...

		pm	pm	pm	pm	pm
Bolton, Howell Croft	dep.	...	11 6	...	...	1115
Four Lane Ends	,,	1117	1120	1120	...	1129
Atherton, Punch Bowl	,,	1128	1131	1121	1134	1140
Atherton, Depot	,,	1132	1135	1135	1138	1144
Leigh, Spinning Jenny Street	arr.	...	...	...	...	...

Railway Stations See Page 89

→ 78. Passing St Michael and All Angels Church at Howe Bridge is no 71. The railway station is in the far background. (JS King)

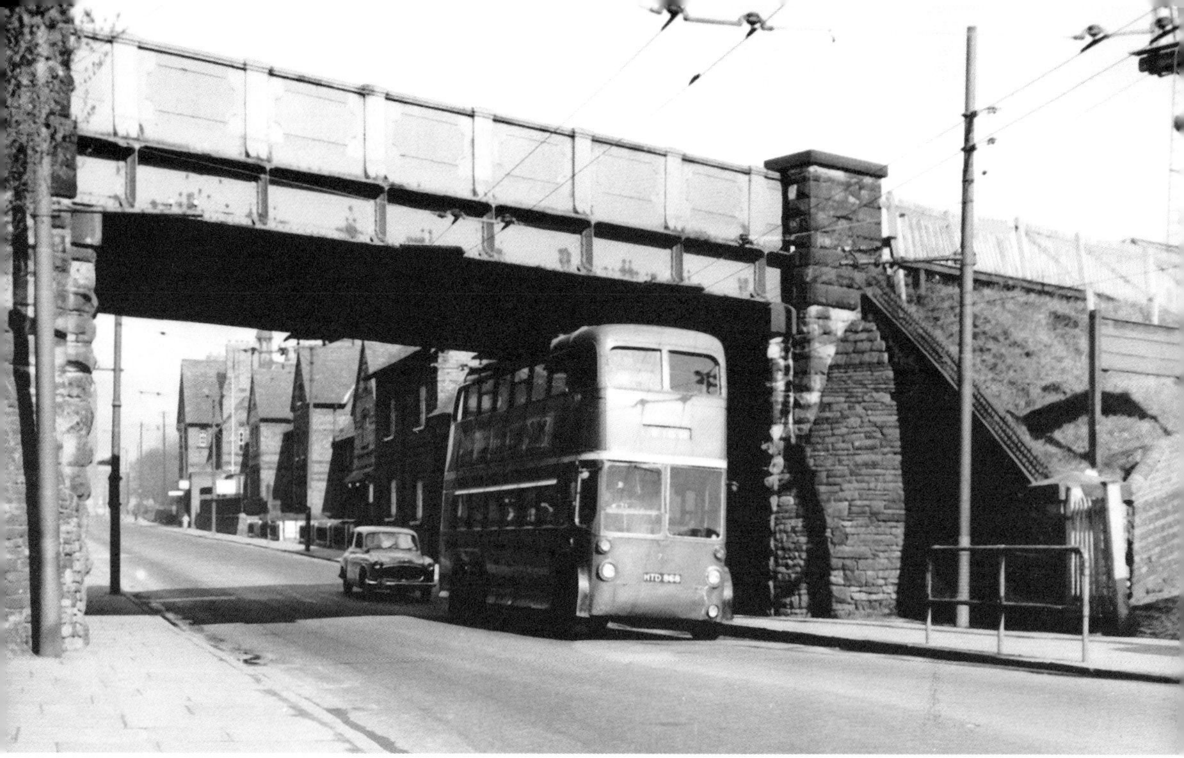
HTD 868

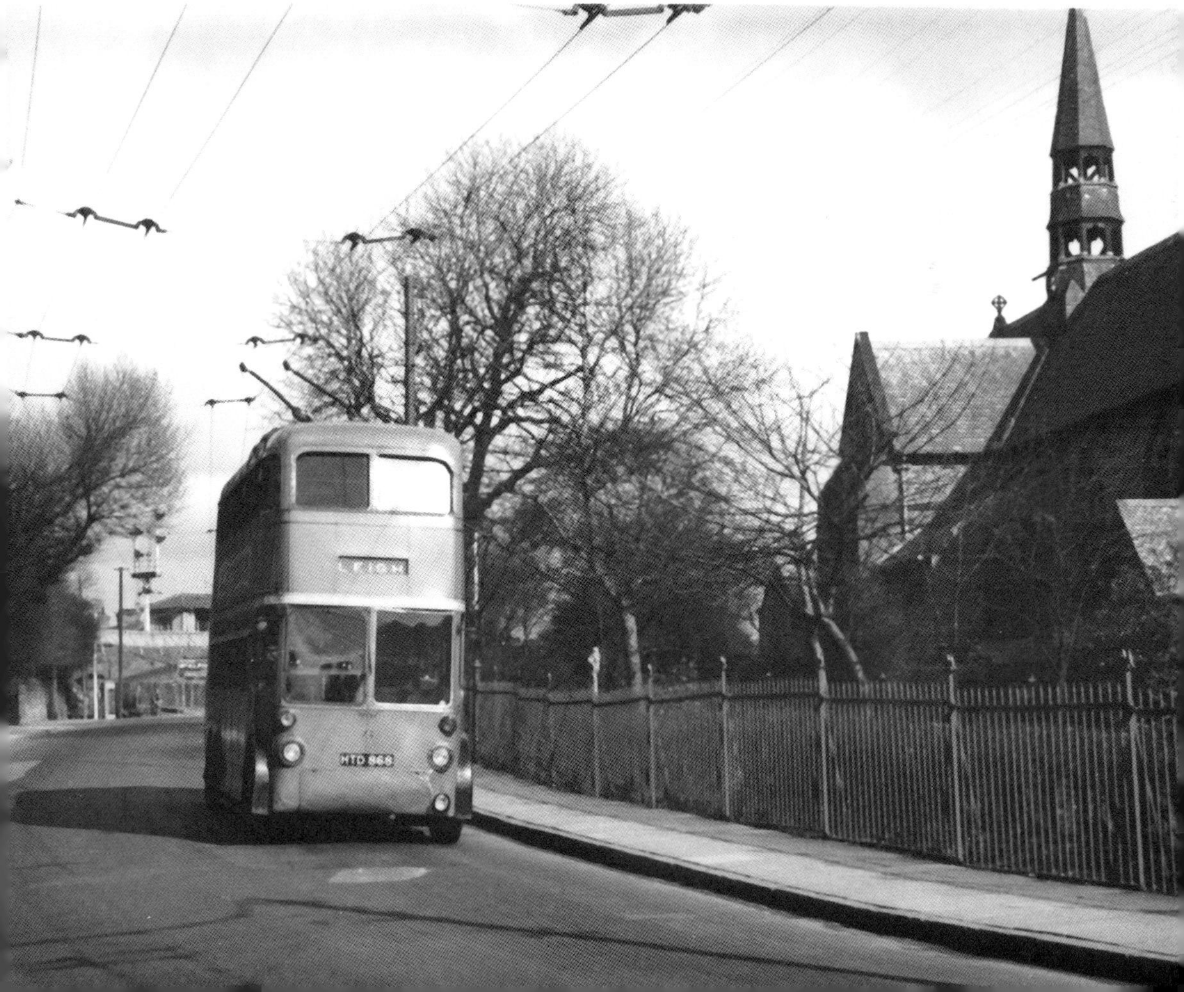
LEIGH
HTD 868

LEIGH
DTC 264
EWS

NO ENTRY
EXCEPT FOR
TROLLEY BUSES
LEIGH
EWS

← 79. Howe Bridge was the location of the head office, depot, and power station of SLT and LUT. The head office and trolleybus depot were on the west side of Leigh Road (on the left of this view), with the LUT motorbus garage on the east side. Known as Atherton Depot, trolleybuses allocated here operated on the Leigh services and some workings on the Swinton / Farnworth route. Seen passing the office building is Leyland no 57, with LUT motorbuses in view outside their garage. The wiring connections leading to the trolleybus depot are evident. (Roy Brook)

← 80. The trolleybus depot was situated behind, and parallel to the office building. Access to Leigh Road was by a short roadway beside the offices where four-wheel Guy no 33 is seen parked on 6th August 1957. The power station cooling tower dominates the background. Note the 'No entry except for trolley buses' sign on the left hand gate post, the tubular suspension of the overhead (ie a metal arm across both sets of wires) above the vehicle, and the wartime markings on the side of the building; EWS stood for Emergency Water Supply. (R Marshall)

81. 1937 built Leyland no 52 has just left the depot to enter service from Leigh on the Mosley Common route. (P Caunt)

BOLTON
61
FTD 453

ODEON
LITTLEWOODS
HTD 868
Stringfellows
SINGERS SEWING CENTRE

← 82. At Atherleigh, on the outskirts of Leigh, 'utility' no 61 is seen en route to Bolton. Road improvement work here in early 1958 necessitated some temporary re-adjustment of the overhead wiring as can be seen in the background. This wiring was never properly re-instated due to the impending closure of the system. (P Mitchell)

← 83. The route in Leigh town centre was via the Market Place, Market Street and King Street. Karrier / Sunbeam no 71 is seen at Leigh Market Place, about to enter Market Street. In the left background, beside the Odeon Cinema (formerly the Hippodrome), can be seen a blue Leigh Corporation bus which has just entered The Avenue. (JS King)

84. Just beyond the Regal Cinema in King Street, the trolleybuses turned left to reach the Spinning Jenny Street terminus. Guy no 13 is seen making this manoeuvre on the Mosley Common service. (JS Cockshott)

85. The alighting stop was outside the side entrance to the Regal Cinema, where Guy no 20 is seen. (P Mitchell)

86. This general view of the Spinning Jenny Street 'LUT Bus Station' is dated 2nd May 1954. It shows 1936 Leyland no 48, in rebuilt form with new front waiting to depart for Bolton. Despite the sign over the enquiry office, the main use of this station was the SLT trolleybus services. The name 'Spinning Jenny' commemorates an 18th century apparatus that revolutionised the cotton industry. It is said to have been invented by Thomas Highs, a native of Leigh. (J Copland)

87. When the Leigh to Mosley Common service became 'all-day' after the war, a loop in the wiring was installed, and the Mosley Common vehicles used the outer wires. This gave opportunities to compare vehicles side by side, as seen here. 1936 Leyland no 51 is seen beside Guy six-wheeler no 30, the final one of the batch. Note the difference in livery, no 30 being in all-over red with grey roof, a short lived style adopted in 1950. (J Fozard)

88. A nice portrait of 'utility' no 60 at Spinning Jenny Street, waiting to depart for Bolton on the last Saturday of operation. A mother and child scramble aboard for what may be their last SLT trolleybus ride. (J Kaye)

89. Leyland no 56 departs from Spinning Jenny Street at the start of its 7½ mile journey to Bolton. (JS Cockshott)

NORTH TO BOLTON

90. The run from Atherton to Bolton was 5⅓ miles long, and trolleybuses ran to a basic 8 ½ minute headway, strengthened by the local Bolton service to Hulton Lane which was sometimes extended to Four Lane Ends. Seen approaching the 'Bacca Shop' junction in Atherton is 'utility' Karrier no 65, which is passing the 'Concert Inn' at the junction of Bolton Road and High Street. Note the motorcyclist without a crash helmet on the right – not illegal in those days. (P Mitchell)

91. A scene in Bolton Road near the 'Queens Arms'. 'Utility' no 62 pulls away from the stop here as it approaches Atherton town centre. (Roy Brook)

92. Just further north, the route crossed the railway near Atherton Central station. Here Guy six-wheeler no 27 is seen on the bridge whilst operating a journey terminating at Atherton. Following the delivery of the post-war trolleybuses, Guy vehicles rarely worked on the Bolton to Leigh service, but did appear on Atherton to Bolton extra journeys (and Atherton to Leigh journeys) at peak hours and Saturdays. Note the small boy sitting on the bridge parapet on the right – no doubt watching the steam trains. (Roy Brook)

93. From Atherton station the route climbed gently through Over Hulton towards Four Lane Ends. On Newbrook Road, a road lined with suburban semis, is Karrier / Sunbeam no 68, seen descending towards Atherton. Note the rather dented front dash panel.
(P Mitchell)

➜ 94. At Four Lane Ends there was a reversing triangle beside the 'Hulton Arms'. This was principally used by the local service from Bolton, although it could also be used from the Atherton direction. Following the demise of the Bolton locals in 1956, the reverser was retained for short workings and learner duties. In this view, dating from after the local trolleybus service had finished, Leyland no 56 is bound for Leigh whilst a trolleybus replacement Bolton motorbus can be seen on the left under the reverser wires. (JS King)

➜ 95. Seen using the reverser on driver training duties on 28th May 1958, just three months before the end of the system, is Karrier / Sunbeam no 71. It is seen pulling forward onto the main road to return towards Atherton. Note that 'Depot' is shown on the destination blind, a consequence of there being no provision on SLT blinds to display 'Special' or 'Reserved'. (PJ Thompson)

NALL WHITLEY
ILTON ARMS
CATERED FOR
A579
A6
A6
OPEN
LEIGH
DTC 265
They come out best on
Kodak
FILM

L

96. Karrier / Sunbeam no 70 is using a newly constructed lay-by at Four Lane Ends, opposite the reversing triangle. (Roy Brook)

➔ 97. After crossing the A6 road at Four Lane Ends, SLT trolleybuses commenced running under wiring owned and maintained by Bolton Corporation. Karrier / Sunbeam no 71, seen at the junction traffic lights, is standing below the section breakers which marked the division between each undertaking's wiring. Note the 'Bolton' boundary sign on the left, between the Police emergency telephone and the telephone kiosk. (Roy Brook)

➔ 98. At the junction of St Helen's Road and Hulton Lane there was a turning circle for the local service operated on behalf of Bolton Corporation. Here, 1937-built Leyland no 53 stands in the circle at the end of its journey from Bolton Bus Station. Note how the road surface has worn away to the left of the vehicle revealing the stone setts. This was due to the continual scrubbing of the surface by the rear wheels of the trolleybuses as they turned. It was rare to see anything other than the Leyland vehicles working the Bolton locals. (J Batty / Online Transport Archive)

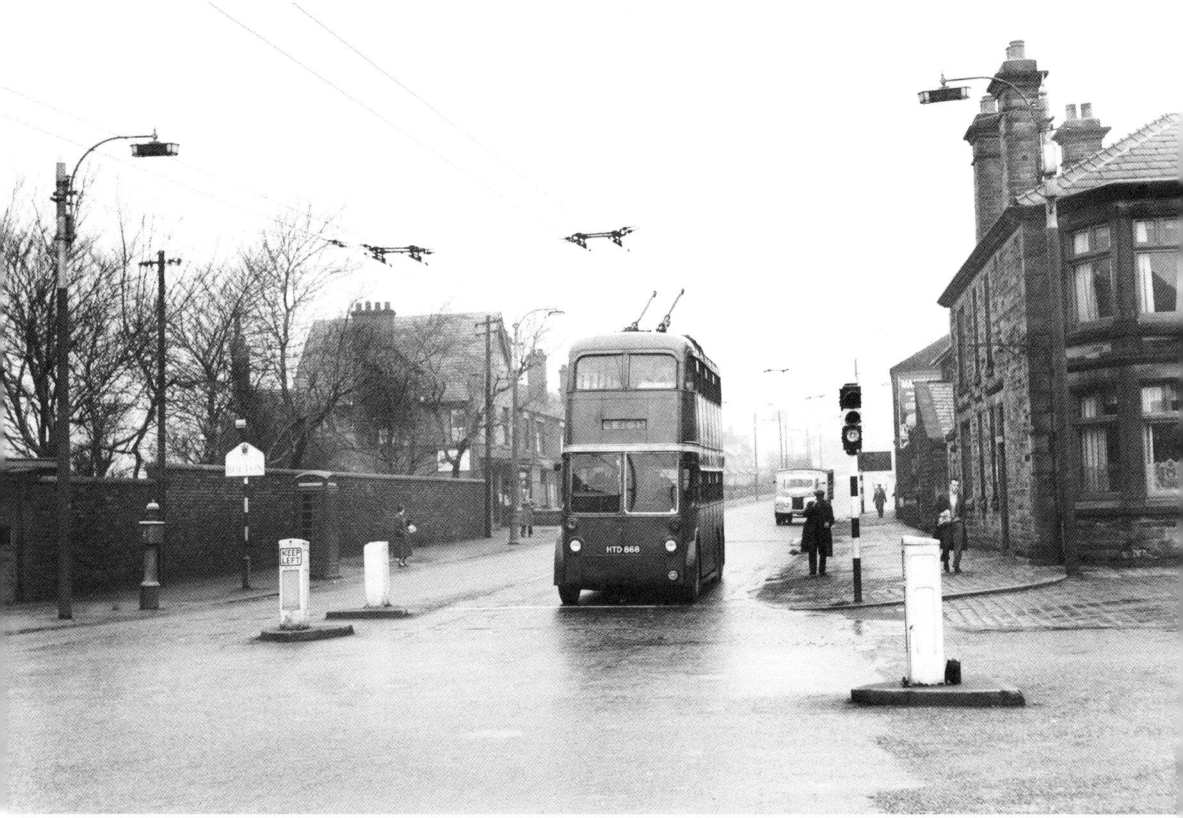
KEEP LEFT
HTD 868

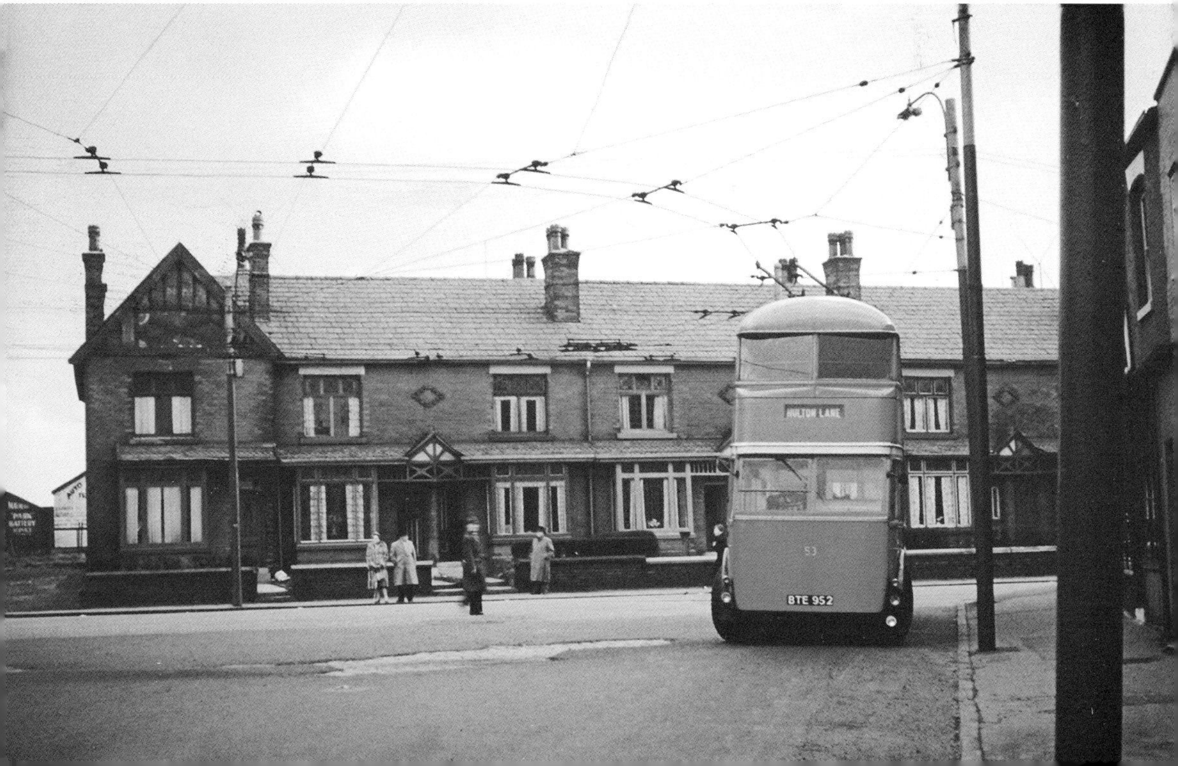
HULTON LANE
53
BTE 952

99. The route descended into Bolton via St Helens Road and Derby Street, in the district of Daubhill. Seen making the ascent out of Bolton in Derby Street is Leyland no 56. Note the municipal style neatness of the Bolton owned wiring compared with the make-do-and-mend appearance of SLT's own. (P Mitchell)

100. At Bolton town centre, the trolleybuses were routed via a one-way clockwise loop from Derby Street via Moor Lane and Ashburner Street to reach Howell Croft bus station. Leyland no 56 is turning from Moor Lane into Ashburner Street, with passengers on the platform step ready to alight. The destination blind has already been changed for the return journey. (J Copland)

101. After leaving the alighting stop in Ashburner Street, trolleybuses made a 'dog-leg' turn into the bus station, a diversion introduced in 1948. 'Utility' no 64 makes this turn alongside the Magee, Marshall brewery warehouse. (P Caunt)

102. A view of the rear of 1937 Leyland no 52 at the Leigh stand in the bus station. On the right is a Bolton Corporation motorbus. (DF Parker)

TUROG - your bread's better!
FOUR LANE ENDS
52
BTE 951

VERNONS
ATE 792

← 103. The stand for the Bolton local service was further along the platform. Leyland no 52 is seen here working to Four Lane Ends, whilst in the rear is similar vehicle no 50 showing 'Depot'. The tower of Bolton Town Hall dominates the background. (Roy Brook)

← 104. A portrait of 1936 Leyland no 48 at the Hulton Lane stand. This vehicle was the only trolleybus other than the Guys to be given a complete new front end. (SNJ White)

105. Karrier / Sunbeam no 69 stands in the sunshine at the bus station before returning to Leigh. (Roy Brook)

106. On leaving the bus station, trolleybuses turned right into Great Moor Street. Leyland no 55, full to capacity, is seen here as it commences a journey to Leigh. This vehicle still displays some of its original features, such as the split platform window and the beading under the lower deck windows.
(P Caunt)

107. Shortly after leaving the bus station (the exit to which is visible in the left background, below the church tower), trolleybuses passed Great Moor Street railway station, seen on the right of this view. The station was closed to passengers in 1954. Leyland no 56 is seen heading towards Derby Street, to rejoin the inbound (towards Bolton) wires. (Roy Brook)

THE VEHICLES

108. **1930 – 1931** **1 – 30** **Guy BTX (six wheel)**
Registration numbers:-
TF 2072 – 2081 (1 – 10)
TF 5240, 5241 (13, 17)
TF 5792 – 5808 (11, 12, 14 – 16, 18 – 29)
TF 6951 (30)

These thirty vehicles comprised the original SLT trolleybus fleet, the initial ten being delivered in 1930 to start services. They had Metropolitan-Vickers 90hp motors and Roe bodies seating 60 (1 to 10) or 56 (11 to 30). These were of 'lowbridge' construction with bench seating upstairs. The capacity of the original ten was soon reduced to 56 seats. During the war, the frontal styling was changed to do away with the 'piano-front' effect in order to accommodate roller blind destination equipment. In the late 1940s many of the batch had their bulbous dash replaced with flat panels. Between 1950 and 1955, nineteen vehicles were given entire new fronts incorporating deep windscreens with a pronounced curve towards each side, and most of these also had their lower side panels lengthened. Two vehicles, nos 1 and 7 were more extensively rebuilt with rubber mounted windows throughout. Only two vehicles, nos 2 and 19 remained largely untouched by this modernisation, retaining their bulbous fronts, although no 4, which ran until the very end of the system, was in similar condition except for a replacement dash panel. The first withdrawal was no 21 in 1955, and eleven of them remained in the fleet right up to the final day of operation. Nos 1 to 18 were licensed to operate in St Helens.

The photograph shows no 2 which ran its entire life with little modification apart from the change to the 'piano-front' when fitted with a roller blind destination display. (Authors collection)

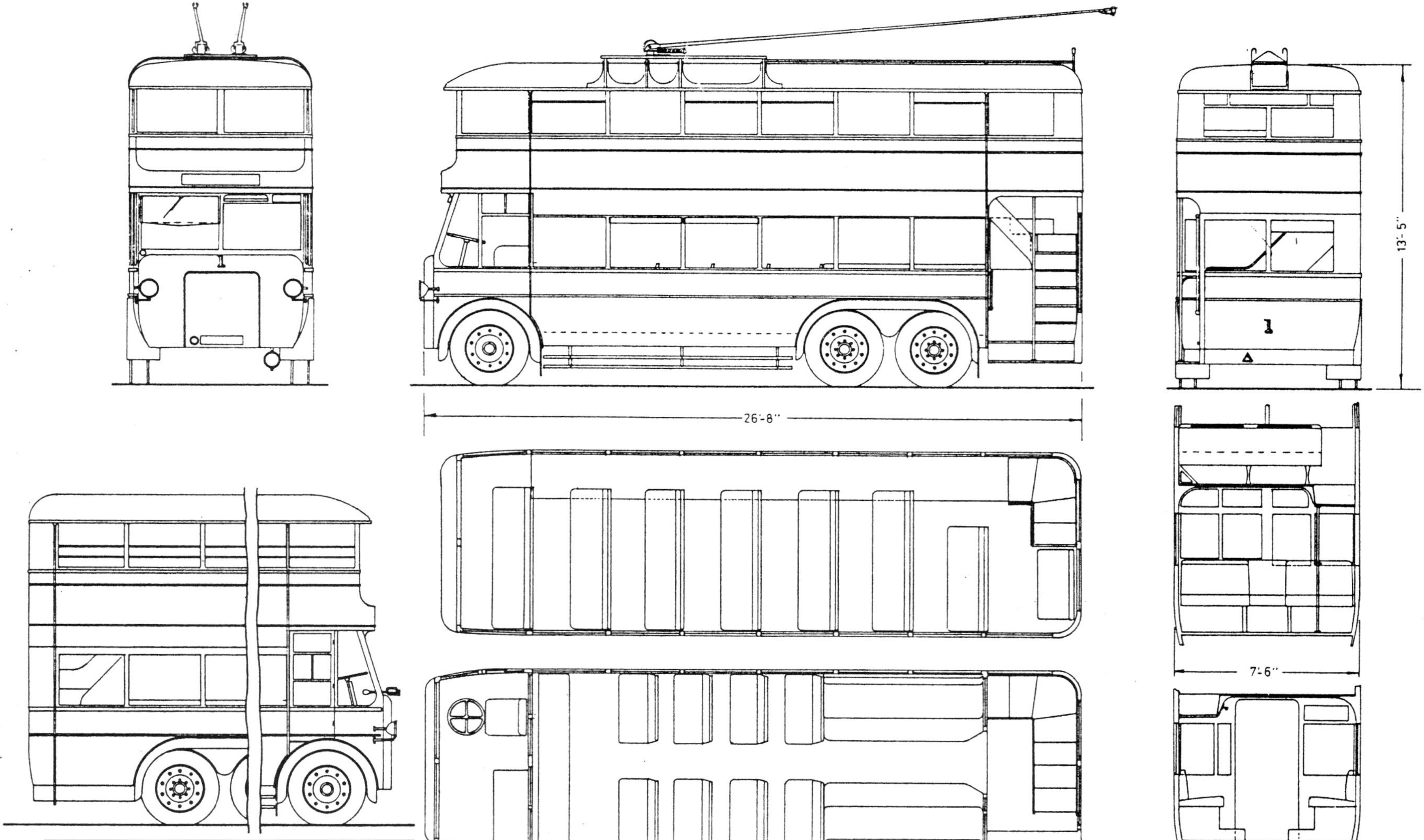

SOUTH LANCASHIRE TRANS.
DOUBLE DECK TROLLEYBUS

TYPE : GUY 'BTX' BUILT 1930	SCALE :
FLEET Nos. 1 to 30 as built.	4mm = 1 Foot

DRAWN BY : TERRY RUSSELL,
HORSHAM, WEST SUSSEX,
ASSISTED WITH INFORMATION FROM K. STRETCH & J. SAUNDERS.

| 109. | **1933** | **31 – 46** | **Guy BT (four wheel)** |

Registration numbers:-
TJ 2969	(42)
TJ 3320 – 3330	(31 – 41)
TJ 3331, 3332	(43, 44)
TJ 3334, 3335	(45, 46)

Delivered for the opening of the Bolton – Leigh service, these sixteen vehicles also had Roe lowbridge bodies, but with a lesser seating capacity of 48. GEC supplied the 80hp motors. The bodywork design differed from the six-wheelers at the front, having a 'v' profile with no 'piano front'. Like their larger sisters, many of these vehicles were modernised after the war, but only six received complete new fronts and of these only two (42 and 44) had extended side panelling fitted. Five vehicles retained the original bulbous front dash panels until withdrawal. The type remained intact until the spring of 1956 when no 36 was withdrawn. Three remained in operation until the end. Nos 39 to 46 were licensed to run in St Helens.

This photograph of no 35 at Swinton shows the 'v' front to the upper deck windows and the bulbous front. Next to the registration plate can be seen the aperture for the tube carrying the bamboo pole, a feature removed to the more conventional position at the rear on many modernised vehicles. (DF Parker)

110.   **1935**   47   **Guy BTX (six wheel)**
        Registration number JW 5370

   Built by Guy motors as a demonstrator in the early 1930s, this trolleybus (with Guy built 56 seat body), came to Atherton in 1935, and was the first highbridge vehicle in the fleet. Guy built many demonstrators (some for foreign use) and 'stock' vehicles in this period, and its full history prior to coming to Atherton is not known. However, its Wolverhampton registration number dated from 1934, and it was operated during that year on loan to Southend on Sea Corporation. Always the 'odd-man-out' in the fleet, it spent its life working on peak hour extras until it became the first SLT trolleybus to be withdrawn in 1951.
   This 1940s photograph shows the vehicle in Atherton operating on a short-working to Tyldesley. The original front dash panel, which curved down from the windscreen, has been replaced by a bulbous type panel. (AF Porter)

111. **1936 -1937   48 – 53   Leyland TTB (six-wheel)**
Registration numbers:-
ATE 792 – 795   (48 – 51)
BTE 951, 952   (52, 53)

Roe again supplied the bodies for these vehicles which had a similar 'v' front to the Guy four wheelers. 64 seats were provided. Electrical equipment was by Metropolitan-Vickers apart from no 51 which had GEC equipment. The 1936 quartet allowed the introduction of the Bolton local service to Hulton Lane / Four Lane Ends, and their purchase was made under a financial arrangement with Bolton Corporation, whereby ownership of the vehicles remained with SLT, at least until the vehicles were fully depreciated. All six vehicles had the bulbous dash panels replaced some time after the war, although in 1954 no 48 was subject to a more comprehensive rebuilding, being the only non-Guy vehicle to receive a complete new front. All the 1936 vehicles were withdrawn in early 1956 upon the demise of the Bolton locals, and under the terms of the agreement, they were passed to Bolton Corporation for disposal. Both nos 52 and 53 remained in service until the end of trolleybus operation.

The photograph shows no 48 in original condition at Hulton Lane turning circle. Compare this view with photograph no 104, showing the re-built vehicle. (Authors collection)

112.   **1938**   54 – 59   **Leyland TTB (six-wheel)**
Registration numbers:-
DTC 261 – 266

Six additional Leyland six-wheelers joined the fleet in 1938, these also having Roe 64 seat bodies, but to a more modern streamlined design, visually similar to the bodies on Karrier chassis being delivered to Doncaster about this time. Metropolitan-Vickers supplied the motors, rated at 90hp. After the war the bodies were tidied up, with beading removed on the lower body sides, the large rear platform window renewed with a smaller unit and the front towing aperture removed. This was done on all except no 55, which alone retained these original features. All six remained in service until the end of the system.

This photograph shows nos 55 and 56 standing together at Leigh in their final forms. (Roy Brook)

ATHERTON

DTC 263

113.   **1943 – 1944**   60 – 65   **Karrier W (four-wheel)**
Registration numbers:-
FTD 451 – 454   (60 – 63)
FTE 152, 153   (64, 65)

   SLT received six of the standard 'no-frills' Karrier / Sunbeam W type four-wheelers, which were the only type of trolleybus available during the war. Nos 60-63 came in 1943 and had GEC 80hp motors, whilst nos 64 and 65 new in 1944, had English Electric 80hp motors All had Weymann 56 seat bodies to 'utility' specification but had fully upholstered seats unlike some others of this type. They were also the first SLT trolleybuses to have an emergency door at the rear of the upper deck. During the 1950s, they had their dash-mounted side lights moved to the standard SLT position, and all but the final two had the headlamps similarly repositioned. All six remained in service until the end of trolleybus operation.
   No 64 is seen in Bolton bus station still in the immediate post-war livery with grey roof.
(C Carter)

114. **1948**   66 – 71   **Karrier / Sunbeam MS2 (six-wheel)**
Registration numbers:-
HTD 863 – 868

SLT's final trolleybus purchase was a batch of six Karrier / Sunbeam MS2 six-wheelers with Weymann 64 seat bodies, new in 1948. They had powerful Metropolitan-Vickers 115hp motors. In 1947-8, Sunbeam produced 34 MS2 type chassis which were badged as 'Karrier', of which these were the first six. The other 28 went to Huddersfield Corporation. They displayed Karrier badges and had chassis numbers in a new post-war Karrier sequence. Despite this, SLT always referred to them as 'Sunbeams' and licensed them as such. Apart from livery, they were not greatly altered throughout their life and all lasted into the final year of operation, no 67 being withdrawn earlier than the others after sustaining serious accident damage.

No 68 is seen here when new, in the immediate post-war livery with grey roof, at Bolton bus station on a Four Lane Ends working, a rare event for this type of vehicle.
(C Carter)

115.   This interior view of the rebuilt Guy trolleybus no 1 shows the rearward facing bench seat behind the cab. On the upper right is the lowered ceiling a consequence of the sunken side gangway on the upper deck. (P Caunt)

116.   The upper deck of the same vehicle shows the 'lowbridge' seating arrangement and sunken gangway. On the inside of the front dome can be seen the trunking which housed the main electrical cables connecting the trolleybase with the cab controls. On this is affixed the fleet number. To the right, on the cant rail, is displayed the wording 'St Helens licence number 115' (P Caunt)

TESTING TIMES

One of the interesting aspects of the SLT trolleybus system was its use by manufacturers to test and demonstrate prototypes and vehicles destined for other systems, both home and abroad. The proximity of the system to the Leyland Motors factory at Leyland, near Preston, resulted in this company regularly using the SLT wires for test purposes. Examples known to have run under SLT wires are:-

1930   AEC prototype six-wheel double deck type 663T, temporarily numbered 11 in the SLT series and painted in SLT colours.
1931   Leyland prototype four-wheel double deck painted in SLT colours.
1933   Leyland prototype four-wheel single deck.
1933   Leyland six-wheel single deck for Perth, Western Australia.
1935   Leyland prototype six-wheel double deck 'low-loader' type TTL. (see opposite photo 48)
1935   Leyland prototype six-wheel double deck for London Transport (no 384).
1939   Leyland prototype six-wheel chassisless 'twin steer' double deck (later becoming London Transport no 1671).
1951   BUT four-wheel single-deck standee type for Glasgow (no TB35).
1954   BUT four-wheel double deck with East Lancashire body for Colombo, Ceylon.
1957   Sunbeam four-wheel single deck with East Lancashire body for Colombo, Ceylon.

117.   In 1933, three six-wheel Leyland chassis were built for Perth in Western Australia, these having a set back front axle to allow a doorway at the front, together with another at the rear. One of the chassis was tested on SLT wires, as seen here. (Authors collection)

118. Only one of the three chassis for Perth was bodied in Britain (by Park Royal), the other two being bodied in Australia. The completed vehicle is seen here in 1933 under test in Partington Lane Swinton, passing the 'Buckley Arms' just north of Swinton Depot. It is negotiating works to remove the redundant tram track. Note the Estler type trolley base, with the poles mounted one on top of the other. The following vehicle is a Lancashire United Leyland motorbus en route for Pendlebury. (Authors collection)

FINALE

← 119. A view of Swinton depot shortly before the end of trolleybus operation in August 1958. Guy no 28, twenty-seven years old, stands in the doorway, with no 6 behind it. On the left is one of the trolleybus replacement motorbuses ('fuel buses' in 1950s LUT parlance) which were new that year, and also of Guy manufacture. No 28 was the last trolleybus in public service, operating from Farnworth into Swinton depot on August 31st, and immediately afterwards it was transferred under its own power using trade plates to Atherton depot for disposal. (P Mitchell)

120. The final passenger carrying trolleybus on the system was Karrier / Sunbeam no 71, which took part in the proceedings on the day following the closure of the system, Monday 1st September. Bearing the legal lettering 'Lancashire United Transport', because the SLT Co had ceased to exist hours beforehand, it took special guests for a mid-day run from Atherton depot to Leigh. Thereafter, the programme for the guests concentrated on celebrating the new bus services, and no 71 returned to the depot, giving a free ride to the public. This is the vehicle in its commemorative livery, with appropriate lettering. Although re-painted for the occasion, it is evident here that the external advertising was retained on the rear panel and on the staircase corner panel.
(R Boardman)

MP Middleton Press
EVOLVING THE ULTIMATE RAIL ENCYCLOPEDIA

Easebourne Lane, Midhurst, West Sussex
GU29 9AZ   Tel:01730 813169
email:info@middletonpress.co.uk

ISBN PREFIXES - A-978 0 906520 B- 978 1 873793 C- 978 1 901706 D-978 1 904474 E - 978 1 906008

* BROCHURE AVAILABLE SHOWING RAILWAY ALBUMS AND NEW TITLES *

ORDER ONLINE - *PLEASE VISIT OUR WEBSITE* - **www.middletonpress.co.u**

TRAMWAY CLASSICS   Editor Robert J Harley

Aldgate & Stepney Tramways to Hackney and West India Docks	B 70 1
Barnet & Finchley Tramways to Golders Green and Highgate	B 93 0
Bath Tramways Peter Davey and Paul Welland	B 86 2
Blackpool Tramways 1933-66 75 years of Streamliners Stephen Lockwood	E 34 5
Bournemouth & Poole Tramways Roy C Anderson	B 47 3
Brightons Tramways The Corporation's routes plus lines to Shoreham and to Rottingdean	B 02 2
Bristol's Tramways A massive system radiating to ten destinations Peter Davey	B 57 2
Burton & Ashby Tramways An often rural light railway Peter M White	C 51 2
Camberwell & West Norwood Trys including Herne Hill and Peckham Rye	B 22 0
Chester Tramways Barry M Marsden	E 04 8
Chesterfield Tramways a typical provincial system Barry Marsden	D 37 1
Clapham & Streatham Tramways including Tooting and Earlsfield J.Gent & J.Meredith	B 97 8
Croydons Tramways J.Gent & J.Meredith including Crystal Palace, Mitcham and Sutton	B 42 8
Derby Tramways a comprehensive city system Colin Barker	D 17 3
Dover's Tramways to River and Maxton	B 24 4
East Ham & West Ham Trys from Stratford and Ilford down to the docks	B 52 7
Edgware & Willesden Tramways including Sudbury, Paddington & Acton	C 18 5
Embankment & Waterloo Trys including the fondly remembered Kingsway Subway	B 41 1
Enfield and Wood Green Tramways Dave Jones	C 03 1
Exeter & Taunton Tramways Two charming small systems J B Perkin	B 32 9
Fulwell - Home for Trams, Trolleys and Buses Professor Bryan Woodriff	D 11 1
Gosport & Horndean Tramways Martin Petch	B 92 3
Great Yarmouth Tramways A seaside pleasure trip Dave Mackley	D 13 5
Hammersmith & Hounslow Trys branches to Hanwell, Acton & Shepherds Bush	C 33 8
Hampstead & Highgate Trys from Tottenham Court Road and King's Cross Dave Jones	B 53 4
Hastings Tramways A sea front and rural ride	B 18 3
Holborn & Finsbury Trys Angel-Balls Pond Road - Moorgate - Bloomsbury	B 79 4
Huddersfield Tramways the original municipal system Stephen Lockwood	D 95 1
Hull Tramways Level crossings and bridges abound Paul Morfitt & Malcolm Wells	D 60 9
Ilford & Barking Tramways to Barkingside, Chadwell Heath and Beckton	B 61 9
Ilkeston & Glossop Tramways Barry M Marsden	D 40 1
Ipswich Tramways Colin Barker	E 55 0
Keighley Tramways & Trolleybuses Barry M Marsden	D 83 8
Kingston & Wimbledon Trys incl Hampton Court, Tooting & four routes from Kingston	B 56 5
Liverpool Tramways - 1 Eastern Routes	C 04 8
Liverpool Tramways - 2 Southern Routes	C 23 9
Liverpool Tramways - 3 Northern Routes A triliogy by Brian Martin	C 46 8
Llandudno & Colwyn Bay Tramways Stephen Lockwood	E 17 8
Lowestoft Tramways a seaside system David Mackley	E 74 1
Maidstone & Chatham Trys from Barming to Loose and from Strood to Rainham	B 40 4
Margate & Ramsgate Tramways including Broadstairs	C 52 9
North Kent Tramways including Bexley, Erith, Dartford, Gravesend and Sheerness	B 44 2
Norwich Tramways A popular system comprising ten main routes David Mackley	C 40 6
Nottinghamshire & Derbyshire Try including the Matlock Cable Tramway Barry M Marsden	D 53 1
Portsmouth Tramways including Southsea Martin Petch	B 72 5
Plymouth and Torquay Trys including Babbacombe Cliff Lift Roy Anderson	E 97 0
Reading Tramways Three routes - a comprehensive coverage Edgar Jordon	B 8
Scarborough Tramway including the Scarborough Cliff Lifts Barry M Marsden	E 1
Seaton & Eastbourne Tramways Attractive miniature lines	B 7
Shepherds Bush & Uxbridge Tramways including Ealing John C Gillham	C 2
Southampton Tramways Martin Petch	B 3
Southend-on-Sea Tramways including the Pier Electric Railway	B 2
South London Tramways 1903-33 Wandsworth - Dartford	D
South London Tramways 1933-52 The Thames to Croydon	D 8
Southwark & Deptford Tramways including the Old Kent Road	B 3
Stamford Hill Tramways including Stoke Newington and Liverpool Street	B 8
Triumphant Tramways of England Stephen Lockwood **FULL COLOUR**	E 6
Twickenham & Kingston Trys extending to Richmond Bridge and Wimbledon	C 3
Victoria & Lambeth Tramways to Nine Elms, Brixton and Kennington	B 4
Waltham Cross & Edmonton Trys to Finsbury Park, Wood Green and Enfield	C 0
Walthamstow & Leyton Trys including Clapton, Chingford Hill and Woodford	B 6
Wandsworth & Battersea Trys from Hammersmith, Putney and Chelsea	B 6
York Tramways & Trolleybuses Barry M Marsden	D 8

TROLLEYBUSES (all limp covers)

Birmingham Trolleybuses ... David Harvey	E
Bournemouth Trolleybuses ... Malcolm N Pearce	C
Bradford Trolleybuses ... Stephen Lockwood	D
Brighton Trolleybuses ... Andrew Henbest	D
Cardiff Trolleybuses ... Stephen Lockwood	D
Chesterfield Trolleybuses ... Barry M Marsden	D
Croydon Trolleybuses ... Terry Russell	B
Darlington Trolleybuses ... Stephen Lockwood	D
Derby Trolleybuses ... Colin Barker	C 7
Doncaster Trolleybuses ... Colin Barker	E
Grimsby & Cleethorpes Trolleybuses ... Colin Barker	D
Hastings Trolleybuses ... Lyndon W Rowe	B
Huddersfield Trolleybuses ... Stephen Lockwood	C
Hull Trolleybuses ... Paul Morfitt and Malcolm Wells	D
Ipswich Trolleybuses ... Colin Barker	D
Maidstone Trolleybuses ... Robert J Harley	C
Manchester & Ashton Trolleybuses ... Stephen Lockwood	E7
Mexborough & Swinton Trolleybuses ... Colin Barker	E
Newcastle Trolleybuses ... Stephen Lockwood	D
Nottinghamshire & Derbyshire Trolleybuses ... Barry M Marsden	D
Portsmouth Trolleybuses ... Barry Cox	C
Reading Trolleybuses ... David Hall	C
South Lancashire Trolleybuses ... Stephen Lockwood	F
South Shields Trolleybuses ... Stephen Lockwood	E
Southend Trolleybuses ... Colin Barker	F
Tees-side Trolleybuses ... Stephen Lockwood	D
Wolverhampton Trolleybuses 1961-67 ... Graham Sidwell	D
Woolwich and Dartford Trolleybuses ... Robert J Harley	B